CULTURE TRUMPS RELIGION, EVERY TIME
The Ethno-Cultural Challenge for the Church

Dr. Oliver Raphael Phillips

Published by New Horizons 21
Orlando, Florida
www.newhorizons21.com

All rights reserved. No part of this publication may be reproduced, stored in a retrieval system, or transmitted in any form or by any means – for example, electronic, photocopy, and recording – without the prior permission of the publisher. The only exception is brief quotations in printed reviews.

Copyright © 2013 -- Dr. Oliver R. Phillips
All rights reserved

ISBN-10:
1481994611

ISBN-13:
9781481994613

Oliver Phillips is available as a speaker on the themes of this book. He can be reached at:
e-mail: oliverrphillips@aol.com

Oliver Phillips is also the author of:
1. The God of a Second Chance
2. Paraparochial Paradigms for Ministry
3. Katrina: Faith, Family, Friends (co-author, Fletcher Tink)
4. E Pluribus Unum: Challenges and Opportunities in Multicultural Ministries
5. How to Sponsor and Nurture an Ethnic Church: Without Losing Your Mind (co-author, Fletcher Tink)
6. The Power of One: A Sermonic Sojourn into a Pluralist World

CONTENTS

ACKNOWLEDGMENTS v

FOREWORD vii
By Tom Nees

INTRODUCTION xi

CHAPTER ONE   DEFINING CULTURE 1

CHAPTER TWO   MAJOR SHIFTS IN IMMIGRATION PATTERNS 9

CHAPTER THREE   CULTURE THROUGH THE EYES OF THE BIBLE 27

CHAPTER FOUR   JESUS – A FIRST CENTURY CULTURAL ICON 39

CHAPTER FIVE   THE EARLY CHURCH CONFRONTS CULTURE 49

CHAPTER SIX   THE HOMOGENOUS UNIT PRINCIPLE (HUP) 61

CHAPTER SEVEN   THE 5-5-5 MISSIONAL STRATEGY FOR STARTING ETHNIC CHURCHES 73

CHAPTER EIGHT   A MISSIONAL BREAKTHROUGH – THE IMMIGRANT CHURCH 87

CHAPTER **NINE**	CQ – THE JOURNEY FROM THEORY TO CONCEPT	107
CHAPTER **TEN**	CQ 101 – BRIDGING THE CULTURAL DIVIDE	121
CHAPTER **ELEVEN**	THE FUTURE OF CULTURAL INTELLIGENCE	159
CHAPTER **TWELVE**	BECOMING CULTURALLY INTELLIGENT	173

ACKNOWLEDGMENTS

I am deeply indebted to Dr. David Livermore, director of the Cultural Intelligence Center, whose passion for CQ has inspired me to enter this fascinating journey of understanding the differences in cultures and how to become culturally competent in working cross-culturally. I was introduced to David's groundbreaking book, Leading with Cultural Intelligence (2009 - ISBN-10: 0814414877) and subsequently became certified as a facilitator for presenting CQ Enhancement Seminars.

Decades ago, Dr. Tom Nees embarked on a quest to bridge the cultural divide that existed in his world of compassion and social justice. His tireless crusade to minister to the marginalized and underserved has always been grounded in his conviction that we must first take the time to exegete the contours of one's culture that reside below the surface. Cultural awareness has opened doors into the cultures with which Tom sought to minister.

Coordinators and directors of the Strategic Readiness Teams of Multicultural Ministries in the Church of the Nazarene have been my tutors. Through countless discourses with these leaders I have been taught by them that each people group possesses values and cultural convictions that transcend their religious loyalties.

My present place of ministry as the lead connector of the Lake Como Connexions Nazarene Church became my research laboratory. As the congregation transitioned from a mono-cultural maintenance stronghold, new congregants brought a multicultural dimension to everything we attempted to do.

My wife, Jean granted me the time to devote to this project.

FOREWORD

Dr. Tom Nees

Cultural diversity and inclusion have become Oliver Phillips' life's work. It began in his Trinidad homeland, part of the larger Caribbean world with its rich mixture of European, African, Indian and indigenous people groups. As an immigrant black man in the United States he quickly absorbed the African American experience and in some ways made it his own without abandoning his Caribbean roots and his growing interest in the mosaic of multicultural America.

He has become an advocate for cultural awareness, indeed for celebrating the unique contribution of all those who came to the Americas on their own or in chains. As a preacher of the Gospel he is most interested in how the Christian church and individual congregations develop their own cultural identities either in harmony with the Scriptures, or, more often than not, as in the theme of this book, how the church and churches mirror the values and behaviors of society often contrary to their own stated beliefs.

Multicultural congregations are rare. Especially if multicultural is narrowly defined as a congregation in which there is no majority group. Gerado Marti, in his recent book, "Worship Across the Racial Divide," defines a multicultural congregation as one in which at least 20 percent of the people are other than the majority group. That broader description includes many more, and as he contends, a growing number of congregations.

The cultural challenge for any congregation with a dominant group is the willingness, if not a desire to become a minority group. Whites are usually unwilling to do so. The tipping point, triggering white flight is usually when trends indicate that sometime in the near future they will not have the majority privilege.

For some so-called minority ethnic groups, the church has become the one place where they are not in the minority, and do not have to accommodate to the dominant culture. Thus black churches became the place where African Americans, excluded from attending white churches, were free to worship as they pleased and follow their own leaders. Hispanics now America's largest ethnic and language minority group are driving the fastest growing segment of U.S. Christianity. While most Hispanic churches are bi-lingual, in worship they prefer the familiar sounds and songs of their native tongue.

It's not that mono-cultural churches are necessarily culturally exclusive, although they may be. It's just that in their desire to advance their Christian faith within the culture and language in which they have come to faith, they tend to remain narrowly defined by their own culture.

The question is, are mono-cultural congregations more cultural than Christian, if the mission of the church is to "actualize the universality of God's kingdom on earth," as Martin Luther King believed? He went on to say that "The church must remove the yoke of segregation from its own body." Inspired by that prophetic call, Gerardo Marti believes that "church leaders today are tired of bearing the embarrassment of having mono-cultural fellowships in an increasing multicultural world."[1]

Oliver Phillips has a lofty vision, to advance an inclusive Christian culture where sub-cultures are welcome and celebrated for their unique contributions to the Kingdom of God in a global village. He calls this cultural intelligence, learning to recognize, respect, and embrace differences. He is seeking to encourage a new Christian community within which various cultures become bridges rather than barriers to the common good.

INTRODUCTION

Culture Trumps Religion, Every Time is the result of a journey that began in a small Bible College in Trinidad and Tobago. Most of the professors in this school were missionaries on appointment with the World Mission Department of the International Church of the Nazarene. They were US citizens. For me, it was only one year after my initiation into the denomination that I entered the institution fully confident that I would prepare for a lifelong tenure as a minister or pastor, with the entire rights and privileges attendant to such a commitment. Students came from Guyana, Barbados, and Trinidad and Tobago. This cultural milieu presented a continuous challenge for me because each people group was entrenched into its own cultural peculiarities, some irritating and others very welcome.

In a religious or in my case, Christian, organization my naiveté led me to assume that although students had come from three different Caribbean locations, our common identity as Nazarenes would serve as a buffer against prejudice, bigotry, discrimination, or cultural isolation. It was not long before I discovered that Barbadians are uniquely different from Trinidadians or Guyanese; Guyanese have cultural identities that are vastly different from Barbadians and Trinidadians; and Trinidadians possess a cultural uniqueness that cannot be found in Barbadians or Guyanese. Nazarene Bible College became a marketplace of cultures all vying for attention as one that claims individuality and or superiority. Nazarenes we all were, but cultural differences were always present, not in any ugly way, but with a competitiveness that could not be ignored.

Dating had lines of demarcation, and whenever cultural protocols were ignored it happened with the complete understanding that there was a hidden tension that would have to be managed by a constant affirmation to one's peers that true love was the motivating factor. Even meals served at times of breakfast, lunch, or dinner reminded all of the culinary tastes that were peculiar to each region. Of course, there were some regional tastes that were the envy of all, e.g. no one complained when "flying fish" from Barbados was served, or "pelau" from Trinidad was the dinner. And everyone agreed that Guyanese "paratha and chicken curry" found its special place on the lunch tables.

This tension however, between Caribbean cultures would not be the only labyrinth that students would have to navigate. Much more complicated and potentially troubling were the polarities that existed between the missionaries from the US and the national student population. Two distinct cultures each honed and cultivated thousands of miles apart collided on a 21 acre campus with an honest hope that the common commitment to train students for full time Christian ministry will mitigate any cultural differences that may surge forward with any claim to independent dominance. Sadly, what emerged was a continuous need on the part of missionaries to remind students that the American culture was far superior to the Caribbean culture, and that a parallel to the mission to train nationals to be prepared for ministry was the need to spread the American culture. From my early introduction to this Bible College I found myself immersed in a crusade to disprove and dismiss any such thesis.

On one occasion we hosted a group of students from one of our eight colleges in the US and Canada. When one student rose to declare the group's purpose for making the trip to Trinidad and the Caribbean, he stated, "We are here to represent Christ, and secondly, to spread the American culture." This, to me was the height of national arrogance. My expressed repulsion to this statement was met with a verbal tirade of justification that proved to be shallow and irrelevant. Thus began my quest to dismantle the missionary attitude of national, racial, and cultural superiority.

Much to my chagrin, this attitude had wider tentacles than was first thought. The missionaries on campus were not the only representatives of the denomination who held firm to the superiority of their culture. Outside the campus where missionaries held administrative leadership positions this attitude of cultural superiority prevailed. In desperation I tried to reconcile Paul's dictum that "There is neither Jew nor Gentile, neither slave nor free, nor is there male and female, for you are all one in Christ Jesus." I hoped that religion would trump culture and that because we passionately claimed to be the beneficiaries of the same Christian holiness experience, that we would be treated as equals.

THIS PROVED TO BE A FALSE ASSUMPTION.

Fast forward. Years have passed, and I found myself in 2003 serving as Director of Mission Strategy at the Global Ministry Center for the Church of the Nazarene. A critical part of my responsibility was to develop strategies for evangelism, church planting, and discipleship among ethnic people groups. The vibrancy of the church planting efforts among these groups represented, at least for the Church of the Nazarene, a ray of hope that there was an effort to keep pace with the growth of immigrants coming into the country. For the Nazarene tribe, as with other Evangelical groups, the battle to keep pace with population growth was a dismal failure, and would be for the foreseeable future.

For various reasons, the cutting edge of growth in the Church of the Nazarene in the USA/Canada, in recent years, has been within the immigrant and minority populations. Our churches throughout the nation and especially in the urban contexts are being confronted with both the challenge and complexities of ministry to these groups. If one were to subtract the gains being made among the ethnic people groups, the net gain would be in the negative column. For that reason, among others, we should develop strategies for effective ministry within these groups.

My decision to become the pastor of a small fledging congregation in Orlando, Florida in October 2011 carried with it the hope that we would help an all-white congregation become multicultural. The immediate neighborhood is white mono-cultural, but I knew that the future would not be reflective of the neighborhood. My demographic research indicated that the ripened harvest field would be pockets of people groups within a five mile radius around the church.

Within months new attendees began to visit the church, and they were all non-white. There began an exodus of members who had invested collectively more than two hundred years of ministry. Without warning or explanation, long standing members disappeared beyond the horizons to nearby Nazarene congregations. Taking inventory of the changes we had instituted I became convinced that the changing cultural environment was the most intimidating challenge for the older group. Today, more than sixteen months from my arrival here, only ten members have elected to remain with us, providing an invaluable link to the past history and legacy.

My long held suspicion has now come full circle. Culture trumps religion, every time!

As Nazarenes, we all believe in the divinity of Christ and the promise of His return to this earth someday. But culture trumps religion!

As Nazarenes, we all believe in the plenary inspiration of Scripture and the necessity of individual response to the invitation to accept the salvation that Christ offers, but culture trumps religion. As Nazarenes we all believe that there are three persons in the trinity and that we are born with a sinful nature because of our Adamic connection, but culture trumps religion.

As Nazarenes we all conclude that the church is made up of redeemed persons and that the Holy Spirit is ever present, convicting the world of the need for repentance, but culture trumps religion.

And yes, we all believe that repentance brings justification, regeneration, and adoption, and that entire sanctification is the cornerstone of a victorious life, but culture trumps religion, every time!

I write this book to advance the thesis that regardless of the strong religious and theological chains that hold us together and give us cause to rejoice that we commonly embrace lofty attributes; our different cultures separate us in the most intimate acts of worship. Culture trumps religion every time! There are those who would be quick to quote Martin Luther King's statement that "Sunday morning is the most segregated hour." I am one who has cited this quotation often, not in a prescriptive sense, but merely as a descriptive opprobrium that needs to be explicated by accepting the reality that culture is a challenge to religion. Culture cannot be underestimated. Culture is a sociological reality that needs to find its place in all attempts to form missional communities.

Our task is not to Christianize culture, but to culturize [my word] Christianity and our discipleship posture before a world that is less friendly to religion in this the genesis of the 21st century.

CHAPTER ONE

DEFINING CULTURE

Recently, I was in transit from London, Ontario, having just completed a CQ Enhancement Seminar at a congregation that hosted 28 different nations. While awaiting the arrival of a shuttle that would take me from the International Concourse to Concourse 2, where I would board a plane to Kansas City, I overheard a dialogue between an impatient attendant and a group of Asian tourists, who were seeking directions, due to apparently confusing signage. The attendant, frustrated by the difficulty, finally blurted out, rather tongue in cheek, "I am not always right, but I'm never wrong!" Such comedic arrogance, sadly enough, is often characteristic of attempts to bridge the cultural divide. Culture trumps religion every time is really a troubling expression because too many practitioners of religion are of the opinion that it is the other way around, and that to even consider that culture is a dominant determinant in the practice of one's faith, borders on sacrilege or heresy.

The divide among cultures is not superficial; it's real! The time has come, according to recent U.S. Census statistics, when interaction with peoples from other cultures has become an everyday occurrence, rather than an occasional encounter. Without humility, a good dose of it, it is possible that, rather than closing the gap between the cultures through intentional understanding, one could easily further alienate others, or worse yet, permanently erode the foundational premises that are necessary to achieving the harmony that future partnerships require. Olive oil and water, to cite a metaphor used by Brooks Peterson, do not make naturally for a good mixture; however, when inserted appropriately in a favorite dish, can work wonders to the palate.

Culture, if it is to be cogently appreciated, must be clearly defined. Yet, the truth is that to define culture is also to recognize the existence of a great divide, a tragic gap or chasm that must be bridged. A common mistake made by most attempts is to relegate culture to a geographic location, like West coast, Southern states, Central America, and even to go so far as to talk of Asian, African, or Eastern culture. This is a good start, but culture is much more. Culture is a totality of contributory elements: behavior patterns, values, assumptions, foods, beliefs, music, institutions, and most assuredly, the product of human ingenuity and necessary for survival. This signifies that our environment is shaped and patterned by the whole of human activity. Anthropologist Clifford Geertz notes that our knowledge of culture grows in spurts. He says, "Culture is not inherited like a genetic code. Instead, culture becomes layers and layers added by our society and our surrounding environment."[2] Culture, therefore, is foundational in life. It indicates that we are a tapestry of a transmitted pattern of meanings, embodied in symbols, a system of inherited conceptions expressed in symbolic forms, by which [we] communicate, perpetuate, and develop our knowledge about and attitudes toward life.[3]

I have gathered a litany of definitions that add up to a preliminary handle on culture, but lack the depth that is necessary to unpack the intricacies that are deeply embedded. One important observation that should be embraced is the dual nature of the definition of culture. First, culture is that which is noticeable to the senses, and secondly, culture is that which is hidden to the senses. Here are some of those definitions:

"Most social scientists today view culture as consisting primarily of the symbolic, ideational, and intangible aspects of human societies. The essence of a culture is not its artifacts, tools, or other tangible cultural elements but how the members of the group interpret, use, and perceive them. It is the values, symbols, interpretations, and perspectives that distinguish one people from another in modernized societies; it is not material objects and other tangible aspects of human societies. People within a culture usually interpret the meaning of symbols, artifacts, and behaviors in the same or in similar ways."[4]

"Culture: learned and shared human patterns or models for living; day- to-day living patterns. These patterns and models pervade all aspects of human social interaction. Culture is mankind's primary <u>adaptive</u> mechanism" (p. 367). [5]

"Culture is the collective programming of the mind which distinguishes the members of one category of people from another." (p. 51).[6]

"By culture we mean all those historically created designs for living, explicit and implicit, rational, irrational, and nonrational, which exist at any given time as potential guides for the behavior of men."[7]

"Culture consists of patterns, explicit and implicit, of and for behavior acquired and transmitted by symbols, constituting the distinctive achievements of human groups, including their embodiments in artifacts; the essential core of culture consists of traditional (i.e. historically derived and selected) ideas and especially their attached values; culture systems may, on the one hand, be considered as products of action, and on the other as conditioning elements of further action."[8]

"Culture is the shared knowledge and schemes created by a set of people for perceiving, interpreting, expressing, and responding to the social realities around them" (p. 9).[9]

"A culture is a <u>configuration</u> of learned behaviors and results of behavior whose component elements are shared and transmitted by the members of a particular society" (p. 32).[10]

"Culture...consists in those patterns relative to behavior and the products of human action which may be inherited, that is, passed on from generation to generation independently of the biological genes" (p. 8).[11]

"Culture has been defined in a number of ways, but most simply, as the learned and shared behavior of a community of interacting human beings" (p. 169).[12]

The word culture comes from the Latin *colere*, which means to cultivate. What do we cultivate? We cultivate a product that operates on three levels: (1) behaviors that are learned, (2) ideas that reinforce beliefs and values, and (3) products that reinforce beliefs. Viewed from these three levels, it is safe to suggest that these products reinforce a cultural belief system and arise out of and reflect a set of underlying ideas and values.

In common conversation, the most frequently traveled path to defining culture is the use of metaphors: "culture is like..." Such an approach reveals a plethora of analogies that present a wide array of definitions, leaving one overwhelmed by the scope of culture's tentacles.

For the present, we will use Brooks Peterson's operational definition: "Culture is the relatively stable set of <u>inner values</u> and beliefs generally held by groups of people in countries or regions and the <u>noticeable impact</u> those values and beliefs have on the peoples' <u>outward behavior and environment</u>."[13] Let's take it apart. The inner values are accrued over time, and they constitute the non-negotiable elements of a culture. They are rarely perceptible, but they have been forged by a culture through adaptation and experience. However, they are released like atomic energy in the behaviors that one notices in the culture we encounter. The recognition of the impact of these values can be the answer to building a bridge to the unfamiliar culture.

What are some of those images that describe culture? What are the images that validate and expose the complexity of the cultural gap? They are the quilt, the tree, the iceberg, and the computer.

Culture is like a handmade quilt. A well-crafted quilt is the result of the imaginative genius of human creativity. Each choice of fabric contributes uniquely to the whole; without which, the quilt is incomplete. In every culture, one finds a variety of factors, contributions to the whole that cannot be ignored. There's language, food, spirituality, laws, history, superstitions, customs, economics, politics, religion, education, health, love and marriage, family traditions, community, travel, just to mention a few. The complexity of this finished product we call culture cannot be underestimated.

Culture is like a tree. One thing we know for certain about a tree is that there are parts we can see, and parts that are hidden from the casual observer. Furthermore, trees change from year to year, depending on their environment. They adapt to the supply of rain, sunlight, wind, nutrients, but they remain essentially a tree. No one ignores the importance of the roots of the tree, the necessary pruning of the branches, and like human beings, they have basic needs like shelter, food, clothing, and relationships. Yet, every tree is so different from the tree a few yards away. A gap exists, and the tree would be the first to admit that the oak is not a maple, and the pine tree is not a pecan tree.

Culture is like an iceberg. Even in tropical countries, most persons have a sense of the subtleties of the iceberg. One inescapable global characteristic of the iceberg is that there is a part you see, and a part you don't. The cultural divide is accentuated, because no discussion of a culture can reasonably take place without recognition of the "under the water" phenomenon. The tragedy of most encounters with another culture is to deal only with the part of the iceberg that can be seen, ignoring the 80% that is submerged. Any discussion with persons who anticipate a trip to a new culture, or who interact with individuals in the workplace is couched with the questions, "What do they look like?" "Are they friendly?" "How's the food?" But that is only the tip of the iceberg!

The tip of the iceberg might make for interesting and exciting conversation, but the "below the surface" realities present intractable values that determine behavior and the environment.

Culture is like the computer. Technologically, culture could also be viewed as the collective programming of the mind that distinguishes the members of one group or category of people from others. To put it simply, culture is the software of the mind.[14] On your computer, hardware does not determine the computer's programming; this is accomplished by the downloaded software. The software gives a specific function and a specific type of production to the computer. As such, culture will determine patterns of thinking, feeling, and acting. When culture is viewed as a computer, we begin to get a glimpse of the divide that exists, because of the different software packages that are to be found in every culture.

Everything we do in the future will depend on one word and one word only. And that word is "demographics." For anyone involved in organizational management or leadership development, from agriculture to economics, from technology to geography, from science to biology, from gerontology to religion, from mathematics to aeronautics, or from chemistry to theology. Because of this reality, defining culture is radically important. The success of mission in the US and Canada would be dependent upon whether or not we get an adequate definition of culture.

In various places through this book I would liken culture to various metaphors, but the underlying theme would be that culture is often robbed of its power. And when that mistake is made the results are catastrophic. Culture trumps religion, every time!

CHAPTER
TWO

MAJOR SHIFTS IN IMMIGRATION PATTERNS

The Facts

Without a doubt, immigration to the United States is burgeoning beyond imaginable proportions. By the term "immigrant," we mean "residents", both legal and undocumented, that were born outside of the United States, who now number, according to the 2003 Population Size and Composition Statistics, 33.5 million persons.

The number of immigrants living in American households has risen 16 percent over the last five years, and increasingly, immigrants are bypassing the traditional gateway states like California and New York, settling directly in parts of the country that until recently saw little immigrant activity — regions like the Upper Midwest, New England and the Rocky Mountain States. By far the largest numbers of immigrants continue to live in the six states that have traditionally attracted them: California, New York, Texas, Florida, New Jersey, and Illinois. The fact still remains true: immigrants continue to flood the country in unprecedented numbers.

America has failed to come to grips with the stark reality of this increased immigration. Forrest Gump was right, "Life is like a box of chocolates, you never know what you're going to get." More to the point, the American church has not come to grips with what opportunities and challenges are presented by this giant shift in people groups, guided wittingly by God's hands. The box of chocolates begins to unravel and surprises abound.

Feelings vary about this new phenomenon. What most Americans are not willing to admit is that immigration is the key to current economic growth. Additionally, immigration is also central to future growth, not only because immigration will continue, but also because the children of immigrants today are the labor force of tomorrow.[15] Immigration might also be the key to sustained membership growth in the U.S. congregations. Research has shown that in my denomination, the Church of the Nazarene, from 1993 to 2003, 820 new churches were started. Of that number, 429 or 52.3% were among ethnic groups, mainly immigrants. Furthermore, 218 or 50.8% of the ethnic-specific congregations were Hispanic. This is an encouraging sign, but it should be accepted with an appreciation for the new windows of evangelistic opportunity provided by the coming of immigrants to these shores.

The advent of this surge of evangelistic prospect has touched states that were previously immune to such immigrant explosion. According to a New York Times reporter (2006), Indiana saw a 34% increase in the number of immigrants; South Dakota saw a 44% rise; Delaware 32%; Missouri 31%; Colorado 28%; and New Hampshire 26%. Over all, immigrants now make up 12.4% of the nation's population, up from 11.2% in 2000. That amounts to an estimated 4.9 million additional immigrants for a total of 35.7 million, a number larger than the population of California.[16]

No other topic will consume the minds of sociologists and anthropologists in the 21st century more than the implications of increased immigration. America is presently witnessing major demographic shifts in immigration patterns. At the time of this writing, Congress is embroiled in rancorous debate about the manner in which this country should solve the problem of undocumented immigrants. At the same time, we struggle to understand those immigrants who have made America home through legal channels and processes. Millions have earned permanent residency and have become naturalized citizens in this land of hope and opportunity. America is faced with the demanding task of defining the assimilation matrix that emerges from such circumstances.

This scenario suggests that we revisit the American self-image of English playwright Israel Zangwill in his signature work, *The Melting Pot*. The play, written at the beginning of the 20th century, endorsed by many Americans, presented a utopian vision of America as a crucible that blended all peoples into a new nation, interethnic and interracial, who would build "the Republic of Man" and "the Kingdom of God." For decades thereafter, this play became the social mantra for an America faced with a rapidly increasing immigrant population. In 1908, when the play opened in Washington, the United States was in the middle of absorbing the largest influx of immigrants in its history – Irish and Germans, followed by Italians and East Europeans, Catholics and Jews – some 18 million new citizens between 1890 and 1920.

It was not until 1963 that Nathan Glazer and Daniel P. Moynihan published the volume *Beyond the Melting Pot*, challenging the assumption that there never was a melting pot, did America dare review this vision of ethnic utopia. The publication raised the ire of some who idealized that the melting pot metaphor was a Godly goal to be aggressively sought after. Many felt betrayed.

Then in 1972 Michael Novak published *The Rise of the Unmeltable Ethnics*. In a review of this compilation Bayard Rustin, a prominent black scholar claimed that "there never was a melting pot; there is not now a melting pot; there never will be a melting pot; and if there ever was it would be such a tasteless soup that we would have to go back and start all over again."

As if to add fuel to fire, in the height of the Civil Rights crusade, a Christian clergyperson, Dr. Martin Luther King Jr. reminded America that 11:00 am on Sunday morning was the most segregated hour in America. This poignant observation by King mobilized some Evangelicals to join a crusade to reverse this reality by advocating for a homogenous worship experience that would blend various cultural groups together.

Today, the church community must again grapple with the question of what is the proper expression of a multicultural society. "Multiculturalism," say some, has become the new civil religion of the United States. Yet it is unclear what is meant by "multiculturalism." Welcomed enthusiastically by some, deplored by others, and maligned by many as an overused and tired buzz word, the issues of multiculturalism continue to pose a challenge of classic proportions to American society in general and to evangelicals specifically.

Before one attempts to offer relevant ideas, however, the gravity of the immigration crisis, reaching every corner of society, must be acknowledged.

Consider for a moment these salient observations:

- Asian-American students comprise one-sixth of the student body at Yale, one-fifth at Harvard, and one-fifth of all students enrolled in medical schools in the United States.

- By 2050 the proportion of Hispanics in the US population will double to 24%, while non-Hispanic whites will comprise a mere majority at 52%.
- In New York, Koreans own 70% of the independent groceries, 80% of the nail salons, and 60% of the dry cleaners.
- Between 2005 and 2010 the white population will grow by only 3.2%, the Census Bureau projects. The Latino population will grow at a rate of 14.4%, Asian Americans/Pacific Islanders at 15.4%, and blacks at 6.3%. The growth rate for the overall population during that timeframe will be 4.2%.
- According to the 2000 Census, there are over 30 million immigrants in the U.S., representing 11 percent of the total population.[17]
- One in five children in the U.S. is the native- or foreign-born child of an immigrant.
- Immigrants and citizens live together in families: 85% of immigrant families with children are mixed status families (families in which at least one parent is a non–U.S. citizen and one child is a U.S. citizen).
- Between 1970 and 2000, the naturalized citizen population increased by 71%.[18]

Taken together, these factors indeed reflect a society in which dramatic changes demand a new way of thinking, as well as an innovative way of doing evangelism. The task of understanding the multicultural mosaic and the approach that the community of faith must design are fraught with difficulties caused by outmoded presuppositions. Three premises that have found prominence in discussions of evangelism and church growth could potentially undermine an effective ecclesiology.

The first assumption is that immigrants come to these shores *Tabular Rasa*, with a cultural "blank slate". Many ignore the deep cultural roots that are imbedded in the worldview of immigrants. One is naïve to attempt to assimilate new arrivals into the cycle of mainstream American church life and expect them to shed all past allegiances.

Second, it is often assumed that the attitudinal portal into which immigrants come to America has been unchanged over the past century. This has resulted in misguided notions of assimilation, which unfortunately have become the foundational impetus for church planting strategies. The America to which immigrants have come in these early years of the 21st century differs greatly from early 20th century America.

Third, because of these first two assumptions, evangelism has claimed a "one size fits all" status. Granted, the claims of the Gospel are universal in its core ingredients. However, effective evangelism only takes place when thoughtful consideration is given to cultural particularity. The Donald McGavran (eminent founder of the Church growth movement) adage that people like to become Christians without crossing racial, linguistic or class barriers, though it may be a pragmatic sociological observation, may be a deficient prescription for evangelism.

This chapter intends to decipher the second assumption above about the misguided notions of assimilation, with the hope that a clearer understanding of the new multicultural America might lead to a more open-minded approach to the immigrant mission field. Unquestionably, new immigrants to this country are a source of renewal and vitality.

Watersheds in Immigration Patterns

The challenge for our time is to understand the changes in immigration that have taken place over the past 100 years. It is the daunting task for the church that seeks to be a catalyst for diversity and inclusion, as well as for all those who seek to contribute to the new mosaic that America has become. The attitudes have changed. Americans must not be seduced into thinking that millions of immigrants were welcomed with affection, be their welcome political, economic, cultural, or religious.

There are six significant historical events that amount to watershed moments because they assault the "melting pot" metaphor, for both good and bad. On the surface, they may not appear as potent contributors to changing the context. However, in combination, they have indelibly imprinted the process by which immigrants enter, successfully or unsuccessfully, the American human landscape. These events are: *first, the two World Wars; second, the Immigration Act of 1965; third, the Civil Rights Act; fourth, Affirmative Action; fifth, Dual Citizenship; and sixth, 9/11.*

World Wars I & II

Prior to these world-reshaping battles, immigrants demonstrated great pride in their homelands. An example may be found in attitudes toward pre-war Germans. They boasted of pride in German ancestry, identity, and culture. In states with large German populations, German was taught in the public schools. Indeed, the mind-set of the general public was one of tolerance.

World War I changed this. As nationalism ran high, pinpointing Germany as the enemy, the German language was banned. The story is often cited that the Woodrow Wilson administration was so hostile to the German culture that it renamed sauerkraut "liberty cabbage." This prompted a widespread move that encouraged forced and immediate assimilation into the US population. While this targeted the German population specifically, it had a ripple effect upon all immigrants. Because of widespread animosity towards the German populace, their immigrants felt that assimilation into the American citizenry was the prudent option. Becoming a naturalized American would shield one from being targeted as the enemy.

Similarly, World War II repeated the response toward the Japanese. History testifies to the ugly episode of nationalist fervor that demanded the incarceration of thousands of Japanese. In three West Coast states, Japanese Americans were placed in internment camps. Yet Japanese men joined the Armed Forces serving in the European theatre of war, most notably the 442nd Regimental Combat Team. This, they felt, would prove their loyalty to the United States.

In the midst of confusion and resentment, Japanese-Americans were often left with no option other than rejection of the Japanese culture. Their hyphenated identity quickly gave way to a rush to become naturalized citizens.

These two world conflicts drove immigrants toward a forced assimilation into the US citizenry. Any current discussion about the role of assimilation must take into account these unnatural situations and circumstances. It is true that these adaptations took place three and four generations ago. However, they continue to be significant because some have used these responses as referents for present dialogue.

Immigration Act of 1965

The restrictive immigration laws of the 1920s favored applicants from Northern Europe. In 1965, President Lyndon Johnson signed a bill that dramatically changed the method by which immigrants were admitted to America. This act, also known as the Hart-Cellar Act, not only allowed more individuals from Third World countries to enter the US, including many Asians who had traditionally been barred from entering America, but also addressed a more liberal policy for refugees. Under the Act, 170,000 immigrants from the East were granted residency, with no more than 20,000 per country. 120,000 immigrants from the West, without "national limitations," were also admitted. The new formula in the immigration reform listed seven visa preferences in order of priority:

1. Unmarried adult sons and daughters of U.S. citizens (maximum 20%).
2. Spouses and unmarried sons and daughters of permanent resident aliens (20%).
3. Members of the professions and scientists and artists of exceptional ability (10%).
4. Married adult sons and daughters of U.S. citizens (10%).
5. Brothers and sisters of U.S. citizens (24%).
6. Skilled and unskilled workers in occupations for which labor is in short supply (10%).
7. Refugees (6%).[19]

However, with the passage of this Immigrant Act came "family sponsorships," which afforded preference to relatives of immigrants already residing in the United States. The bill was significant in that future immigrants were welcomed because of their skills/professions, and not categorized by their countries of origin.

Before President Johnson signed this bill, the Senate voted 76 to 18 in favor of this act, with opposition primarily by Southern senators. The House likewise voted 326 to 69 in favor.

The results of the new policies directly affected how immigrants viewed assimilation into mainstream America. The adverse effect was that it resulted in the emergence of geographically concentrated immigrant clusters – Cubans in Florida, Mexicans in California and Texas, Dominicans and other immigrants from the Caribbean in New York --- a move seen by many as threatening assimilation.

This gathering of immigrants however, is not necessarily an unwelcome phenomenon. The traditionalist view has been that any attempt at specific ethnic communities only serves to polarize the immigrants from the American community. Not necessarily! This view fails to appreciate the social capital that is vibrant within these communities. Rather than polarizing, these enclaves serve to teach immigrants how to assimilate without losing their original identity. Such communities help to ease intergenerational and bicultural conflicts. Second generation immigrants often perceive their parents as the "guardians and protectors" of the culture they left behind.

Multiculturalism must now be redefined because immigrant America is not what it once was. The newcomers of the last 35 years are Mexican, Salvadoran, Dominican, Chinese, Filipino, Indian, Korean, Vietnamese, and Cambodian. Altogether, between 1971 and 2000, the United States admitted approximately 21 million immigrants, far exceeding the number who came during the first three decades of the 20th century; but in contrast, more than 80% of them were Latino or Asian in origin. The latest census reports that the U.S. population is 75.1% white, 12.3% Black, 12.5% Latino, 3.6% Asian, 5.5% some other race, 2.4% two or more races.[20]

Civil Rights Act

The date was March 7, 1965, when Congressman John Lewis, then chairman of the Student Nonviolent Coordinating Committee (SNCC), led one of the most dramatic protests of the civil rights movement. Six hundred marchers crossed the Edmund Pettus

Bridge in Selma, Alabama, singing "We Shall Overcome" and claiming their full rights as citizens of the United States. Needless to say, these visitors did not enjoy a hearty welcome; they were greeted by state troopers and local police in a confrontation that has claimed the epithet "Bloody Sunday."

In 2003, on another Sunday morning, 90 immigrants and their supporters, part of the Immigrant Worker Freedom Rides, reenacted the Pettus Bridge march, this time singing *"We Shall Overcome"* and *"Las Mananitas de los Inmigrantes"* and chanting *"Somos Uno/We are One."*

This is no repeat moment that should be shrugged away as an ordinary event. It has serious implications. The new immigrants to the US have discovered that the Civil Rights Act provides them with an umbrella under which they may reside without necessarily assimilating into the mainstream. The rights justly claimed by proponents of civil rights legislation have not been the sole proprietorship of those who aggressively pursued its passage. Prior to the historic Civil Rights Act, it was never conceived that immigrants would necessarily view assimilation as personally non-productive. However, with the myriad privileges that were enacted by this legislation, immigrants chose to co-opt these advantages, placing the need to assimilate on the back burner of secondary importance.

Affirmative Action

The Supreme Court's 2003 decision upholding affirmative action at the University of Michigan and enshrining "diversity" as a compelling national interest only encouraged new Americans to see themselves as being different. This paraphrased observation made in a leading newspaper editorial finally brought to light an issue that has been avoided for the better part of five decades. Major studies of immigration avoided discussing affirmative action. Conversely, most experts agreed that immigrant participation in affirmative action remained the ultimate nightmare of affirmative action.

At the core of all the contention has been the immigrants' understanding that to be different (i.e. racial preferences in affirmative action) was to open the door to opportunities that were prohibited under other circumstances (i.e. restrictive immigration policies).

American immigration has been caught in a puzzle of unintended consequences. The Immigration Act of 1965 collides with the well-intended Affirmative Action policies of the 60's and 70's. As noted earlier, during the 60's and early 70's, most immigrants came to America from southern and eastern Europe. Legal immigration from Latin America and Asia however, increased sharply after 1965. Latin American countries sent 88,400 immigrants to America in 1965, as compared with 113,400 from Europe and another 38,300 from Canada. Significantly, by 1970 immigration from Latin America had grown by 30% to 115,200.

Between 1965 and 2000, approximately 35 million immigrants had come to America. Accordingly, close to 26 million of these immigrants could claim affirmative action preferences on the basis of historic discrimination they had never experienced. This represents a political puzzle for policy makers, but a cultural and economic loophole for immigrants.

Immigrants have become the beneficiaries of affirmative action policies in the job hiring arena in unprecedented proportions. Ethnic networking has been the result of this shift. One can easily observe the tendency for language, kinship, and community ties to convert certain American jobs into immigrant enclaves as is seen in restaurants, hotels, janitorial services, and furniture manufacturing in major cities in the US.

Affirmative action policies have been viewed by immigrants as a *sine qua non* for assessing the set aside programs which opened the doors of opportunity. The result of such appropriation has been a resistance to assimilate into the mainstream without some particular label It is not enough, immigrants would argue, to be an American; it is expeditious to be labeled a "minority" since by so doing doors will be opened.

Evangelicals are often puzzled by the unwillingness of immigrants to divorce themselves from "designated minority" labels. This is a matter of self-interest and economic survival. The gains from embracing the melting pot hypothesis don't seem to balance the beneficence accrued from seeking inclusion into the targets of affirmative action. For the foreseeable future, there will be a continued tension between the historic minorities – Native Americans and African Americans – who consider immigrants' acceptance into the affirmative action dialogue as an unwelcome and intrusive interplay.

That being said, affirmative action, a legislative mechanism designed to offer race-conscious remedies for unjust policies and practices of the past, will continue to attract immigrants to its side.

Dual Citizenship

Exclusive loyalty to the United States was once considered compulsory for anyone contemplating citizenship. Going back to the 1790s, the language in the oath of citizenship conveys such allegiance directly. It states:

I hereby declare, on oath, that I absolutely and entirely renounce and abjure all allegiance and fidelity to any foreign prince, potentate, state or sovereignty; that I will support and defend the Constitution of the United States of America against all enemies, foreign and domestic; that I will bear arms on behalf of the United States when required by law....

This would seem to fly in the face of any attempt to consider dual citizenship. However, the import of these words no longer conveys the same pungent uni-national allegiance. Another example of the propensity for such allegiance could be found in every American passport:

Under certain circumstances, you may lose your citizenship by performing any of the following acts:

1. naturalizing in a foreign state
2. taking an oath or making a declaration to a foreign state
3. certain service in the armed forces of a foreign state
4. accepting employment with a foreign government;
5. by formally renouncing U.S citizenship before a U.S consular official overseas.

Some have suggested that the Supreme Court, in many rulings, seems to have dissected the language of these documents and has rendered them lame-duck instruments for such allegiance.

One should not take lightly the occasion when, in 2001 on Cinco de Mayo, Mexico's national day, President George W. Bush sent a message in Spanish to the Mexican-origin population. Some may argue that it was an astute political ploy on Bush's part and thereby miss the subliminal significance embedded in the action. Dual citizenship is today an accepted option for millions. More than 25 nations presently allow for dual citizenship. In 1998, Mexico amended its Constitution allowing its nationals who became U.S citizens to retain Mexican citizenship. These moves appeared to enable naturalized Mexican citizens to inherit and buy land in Mexico, allow immigrants to protect their interests and rights in the U.S., and furthermore help Mexican Americans to serve as interests groups on behalf on Mexican interests in the U.S.

What this shift in immigration means is that no longer is there an urgent obligation to shed the moorings of one's culture in order to be assimilated into the American culture. One can have the best of both worlds. America drifts further away from the "melting pot myth" by these subtle but inclusive shifts. Forceful assimilation has lost its sharp exclusive edge, and multiculturalism itself must be redefined.

What then, are we to make of the fact that immigrants today maintain such stronger ties than in the past to their homeland and its people? It represents a stark departure from the immigrant kaleidoscope of the early 20th century European patterns. Immigrants today may become American naturalized citizens, but the allegiances to their home remains partially intact. Added to this confusion, the rate at which immigrants have chosen to become citizens has declined dramatically. Naturalization rates of legal immigrant adults, which had been as high as 80% in 1950, fell to 44% in 1990. Even discounting the impact of continuing immigration, this is the lowest rate in a hundred years.

Until this change took place, dual citizenship was looked upon as an incongruity to be eliminated as quickly as possible. Nowadays, many immigrants remain citizens of both countries, with more than 500,000 children born in the United States each year, who by that very fact alone are American citizens, but choose to remain citizens of their parents' countries of origin. It must be noted that this new fad is different from the earlier exceptions of European dual citizenship. Then, dual citizenship was more or less a passive legal status made aware to the immigrant upon a casual visit to the homeland, where one might discover that conscription to the Armed Services is his legacy to be responded to. Today however, dual citizenship is a conscious and deliberate matter accommodating constant contact with friends and relatives through regular visits. Added to this stimulus, many immigrants are encouraged by their countries' leadership to maintain their allegiance, further promoting identification and commitment.

This trend indisputably affects the myth of the melting pot, simply because hundreds of thousands of immigrants keep such close contact with the homeland that they remain internally hybrid, while externally it may seem that they have conveniently assimilated into the mainstream.

September 11, 2001

The effects of September 11 on the immigrant population have been varied and difficult to gauge. As with World Wars I & II, vis-à-vis the Germans, Italians, and Japanese, there was measured bigotry. September 11 is cited as an important trend affecting the melting pot theory, not because it discourages it, but because it places a new twist on what it means to be American.

When the president of the United States visited Ground Zero on Friday, September 14, someone yelled from the crowd that he couldn't hear him, to which Bush responded, "I can hear you. The whole world can hear you. And the people who knocked down these buildings will hear from all of us soon." Immediately the crowd of rescue workers began chanting, "U.S.A.! U.S.A.! U.S.A.!" This crowd comprised Americans of all nationalities, and their unforgettable message was: We are all Americans. Cab drivers from Pakistan, Haiti, Ethiopia, and Latin America, displaying American flags were among those who honked their horns in support of a ready response by the US.

Not since World War II have Americans demonstrated such unabashed patriotism. It would have been an easy ploy for this country to have deteriorated into ethnic disharmony, disunity, and reprisals among immigrant groups. Stigmatizing or isolating any group would have destabilized the very values that immunize all Americans – including those of the Muslim faith or Arab ancestry – against letting ethnic or religious loyalties engulf their bonds to countries of origin.

The events of 9/11 placed America on a defensive path that would affect immigration policy for the foreseeable future. All foreign-born citizens, particularly Arab-born understand quite well the suspicion and unease that have surfaced in America because of the horrendous acts against American citizens. Quite understandably, there was some adverse reaction. However, Americans resurrected a national cohesive spirit of patriotism that has become the envy of many a nation that came unglued because of such a catastrophe.

Interestingly, it is reported that applications for citizenship multiplied in the months following 9/11, well over 60% more immigrants applied for naturalization in that period than in the same period the year before.

Opportunities

From its beginning, America has not been the mythical melting pot but has been marked by its diversity.[21] When 78% of Los Angeles residents are ethnics, and more Jews live in New York City than in Israel, and when Chicago is the second largest Polish city anywhere in the world,[22] it represents a tremendous evangelistic opportunity.

Bible translators insist that people never will be reached effectively for the gospel until the gospel is in the language of their souls. If the church is to reach these immigrants with the gospel, ethnic leaders must be developed. When an ethnic church sponsors a new ethnic church, 98% of the pastors come from that ethnic group. When leaders encourage indigenous leaders to arise within ethnic population groups, the growth of churches of that ethnic segment often doubles.[23]

The greater ethnic diversity will require an understanding of the distinctives of the respective cultures. A key to ministry in the new era will be the creation of multiethnic faith communities that reflect the demographic makeup of their populations.[24]

It seems to me that the crucial aspect of the challenge facing the 21st century church would be the recognition that ministry in this pluralistic culture would require two things. First, people evince different responses to the claims of the gospel. Some people are early adopters, eager to adapt to any kind of change, becoming convinced quickly and wanting to make the necessary adjustments in a new cultural context. Second, it is important to understand people's differing cultural perspectives. Each culture marches to a different drummer, and its peoples themselves sometimes demonstrate different perspectives of the new environment. We must listen to each beat and be culturally sensitive so that we can better communicate spiritual truth.

The Unity in Diversity we Seek

When I entered this country in 1968, I had every intention of being assimilated into the norms, customs, and cultural identifications of these United States. After 38 years, I don't know that I am any closer to being a melted specimen of assimilation. Granted, I arrived with every intention to say goodbye forever to my homeland of 24 years. However, I must be grateful to the soil that gave me birth and a fundamental educational foundation. It is Trinidad that responded to my innate passion to achieve and to strive for the highest possible apexes of life's aspirations.

To this day, after recently having embarked on the U.S. naturalization process, my nostalgia for the homeland is still colonized by the occasional smells, sounds, and acquaintances that remind me of a land 2,469 nautical miles away. This is by no means a reflection on the US, but a testament to the powerful influence that one's culture dispatches to the very core value system and the making of the individual. America, in the "flat world" template, is more of a clearing house for global imagination and capacity. I have become a patriotic participant in the "land of the free and the home of the brave," but as America competes in the global war of ideas she is richer because of the diversity that I bring to its shores. As America has become part and parcel of who I am, I believe that I have in part, made America what it is today.

Interestingly, the America that I met in 1968 is vastly different from the America I know today. America is no longer a monolithic community where the superiority of the Anglo-American culture is proposed. America today has been infected by the incursion of immigrants to the extent that it has become a porous composite of various cultures, each contributing to the subtle changes that have affected the whole. Assimilation is a two-way street. In the long run, America absorbs and accommodates the cultural variety of its new citizens, and on the other hand its citizens convey pride in their ethnicity.

Assimilation was once a clear-cut proposition for many who immigrated to these shores. On the other hand, as has been the thesis of this article, the melting pot has co-opted for a complicated fusion cuisine, one that leaves an unpleasant taste on the traditional American palate.

Perhaps Jurgen Moltman can speak to us all:

> Trust is the art of living not only in what we have in common, but in our differences as well – not merely with people like ourselves but with others too. If in the Christian community common trust springs from the love of Christ, and if it is the fellowship of the Spirit which brings together people who are different, that fellowship will become the source which strengthens our capacity for community in the natural relationships of life.[25]

CHAPTER
THREE

CULTURE THROUGH THE EYES OF THE BIBLE

Without culture, there would be no Bible. However, I must hasten to say that we cannot appreciate and understand the Bible if we remove it from its own context, rather, we have to change our mind-set to better understand the ancient way of life.

I contend that the Bible is not a specific universal treatise about values, impact, and behaviors of different nations throughout history, but it is the panoramic journey of the people of Israel who were never really numbered more than ten million. One must admire the tenacity and perseverance of this people group, but should never lose sight of the uniqueness of the culture whose very nature affect every other culture through the 4,000 years spanned by the Bible. The Bible provides much useful and interesting information regarding the cultures of ancient prophets, peoples, and civilizations - information about their music, language, arts, literature, religious institutions, monetary system, food, clothing, calendric structure, marriage practices, and so forth.

It would be difficult for me to argue that God had a "preferential option" for the people of Israel unless I defend God in what God did at the tower of Babel. The fiasco at Babel found in Genesis chapter 11, has been too often viewed and interpreted as the activity of God that portended a curse by God for the people's arrogance and prideful ambition. It was always the plan of God to have different cultures and races. Although the narrative account of Genesis seems to suggest that the people were of one mind, they were not one culture. The text states, "They said to each other, 'Come, let's make bricks and bake them thoroughly.' They used brick instead of stone, and tar for mortar. Then they said, 'Come, let us build ourselves a city, with a tower that reaches to the heavens, so that we may make a name for ourselves and not be scattered over the face of the whole earth'."

God reacted swiftly by dispersing the people through the introduction of different languages. In my humble opinion, I believe that this served as a blessing to the people in the fulfillment of God's promise towards the salvation of all people groups. Babel is not the place that different cultures began, otherwise we would have to conclude that it is humanity's responsibility to reverse or redeem the punishment. As Randy Woodley notes, the scattering of the people at Babel was in the fulfillment of God's plan:

> God has planned since the beginning of time to cultivate diversity among human beings. When people tried to circumvent His plan, God intervened by creating many languages. ... [God] is a God of innovation and extravagance, diversity and lavishness. God is the artist who formed the planet Saturn and its beautiful surrounding rings. He is the humorist who formed the giraffe and the narwhale, the armadillo and the platypus. God is the designer who set the constellations in place, who causes roses to bloom and who enables bees to make honey. We are not threatened by the stars that tower overhead or by a blooming rose or by the taste of honey in our tea. Should we be so surprised to find that God also created such diversity in human beings—all distinct and all equal—or that He insists that every culture be unique in its own right?[26]

Babel is God's plan to reach all peoples. The church today would be well served by appreciating the vehicle of culture that is critical to the efficacy of the missiologist's task to evangelize the world. Missiologist Andrew Walls contends that one of the great characteristics of the gospel message is its ability to adapt to particular cultural expressions. African theologian Lamin Sanneh suggests that the greatest miracle of the twentieth century is the translation of the Bible into different languages. Culture trumps religion, every time.

It was not long after the Babel episode that we are confronted with the narrative of the call of Abram. Bible scholars are divided as to whether this call was from Mesopotamia or from Ur of the Chaldees, but this is not the platform to decipher this apparent contradiction of mere interpretations. This much could be said however, Stephen, in his account of the call seemed to have a starkly different rendition (Acts 7:2-4) of what really happened as recorded in Genesis 15:7.

However, when a man is willing to lie to protect the purity of his culture, one must give more than scant attention to his motive. Recorded in the twelfth chapter of Genesis is the willingness of Abram to concoct a lie so that his wife Sarai may not be defiled by the Egyptian culture. Sarai was reputedly so beautiful that

Abram believed that she would be a pawn and sexual prey to the men in Egypt.

Abram was willing to protect the culture that he believed his God had mandated him to protect. Listen to the record of the Bible, "Now the LORD had said to Abram: 'Get out of your country, from your family and from your father's house, to a land that I will show you. I will make you a great nation; I will bless you and make your name great; and you shall be a blessing. I will bless those who bless you, and I will curse him who curses you; and in you all the families of the earth shall be blessed'." (Genesis 12:1-3). This was an unmistakable call to cultural exceptionality. A culture was born here. This culture was to be protected and appreciated, at all costs, even if one has to lie to do so.

Following this line of thinking, I am not surprised that Abram was tenacious about preserving this new culture. Everything that followed is the demonstration of Abram's efforts to ensure that his culture would trump every decision that was consequently made.

Shem, Ham, and Japeth were the three sons of Noah, and ten generations later, Abram was born, as the descendent of Shem, by way of Abram's father, Terah. Abram's brothers – Haran and Nahor – never heard from God as Abram did. Yet it is to Abram that the explicit call came to separate from their history and heritage, and become a new culture. This meager beginning must not be overlooked, for it is within this crucible of destiny that the indomitable contours of a culture were to be eternally defined and carved for all to see. More than three hundred times in the writings of the Prophets the name Abram (Abraham) would be mentioned. No other culture in the Bible can lay claim to such a clear call to destiny. All the subsequent machinations of this new people would be carved by this unlimited call to create a culture that would be different from and [superior] to all other biblical cultures.

Trouble was, however, brewing on the horizon for this new culture. The dictum, **"I will make you into a great nation. You will be a blessing...and all peoples on earth will be blessed through you."** (Gen. 12:2, 3) would define the future for this people. For four hundred years the Jewish people would be subject to cruel forms of slavery in Egypt under the harsh and inhumane reign of the Pharaohs. They became the political-economic property of cruel task masters, but as the biblical narratives would suggest, their unique culture remained resilient. Their eventual freedom was attained because their culture trumped all attempts to cultural annihilation.

This nascent account of the early life of a people is significant to this book's thesis because it demonstrates the power of culture, and further substantiates my argument that we are not well served by underestimating the power of culture.

Now the journey begins. Through Moses, deliverance finally came. But the bondage of many years only served to further cement the disparate elements of their culture. They emerged from the tentacles of Pharaoh more united as a people, resolute in their commitment to live out the promises made to Abraham, that they would be a blessed people.

According to an old story, the powerful Prussian King Frederick the Great had a chaplain who was a Bible-believer, though Frederick himself was a rationalist. One day, Frederick challenged his chaplain, "In a word, give me a good argument for the God of the Bible." His chaplain, a knowledgeable man, responded, "The Jew, your majesty!" When, in 1,400 BC, the Jews left Egypt, there was every indication that God wanted a people through whom God could reveal who God is. The record states, "See, I have taught you decrees and laws as the LORD my God commanded me, so that you may follow them in the land you are entering to take possession of it. Observe them carefully, for this will show your wisdom and understanding to the nations, who will hear about these decrees and say, `Surely this great nation is a wise and understanding people'." (Deuteronomy 4:5).

To these new adherents of a new culture, God gave an elaborate set of laws - some moral, some civil, some ceremonial - which also set them apart from the nations around them. Their culture was to be preserved through the observance of laws and the remembrance of their journey.

But that, as the saying goes, was not the end of the story. Israel would be surrounded by other cultures that would occasionally defeat them in battle and besiege their cities, resulting in plague, famine, cannibalism, and starvation. Decade after decade they would be scattered among foreign nations where some would die and others would live in constant fear of both real and imagined disasters, or turn to other gods. They would be exiled and sold as slaves, resulting in a decrease in their population as they suffered from fearful plagues, prolonged disasters, and lingering illnesses.

In the book of Revelation we read, "After this I looked, and behold, a great multitude that no one could number, from every nation, from all tribes and peoples and languages, standing before the throne and before the Lamb, clothed in white robes, with palm branches in their hands, and crying out with a loud voice, "Salvation belongs to our God who sits on the throne, and to the Lamb!" (Rev. 7:9-10). This seems to imply that even on the final convocation of the nations, clear lines of cultural divisions are accepted as normative. They will be gathering around the unified throne with their cultural uniqueness intact.

The intervening years between the Exodus and the final convocation is a continuous validation of my thesis that culture trumps religion, every time. It is in these years that God surrounded Israel with nations, not so that they could be coopted by the culture of Israel, but so that they could benefit from the blessings that God was bestowing on Israel. Wars characterized the existence of these nations next to each other. Israel was always protecting their culture!God surrounded Israel with many cultures stretching from Egypt north to Syria and south through Mesopotamia.

CULTURE THROUGH THE EYES OF THE BIBLE

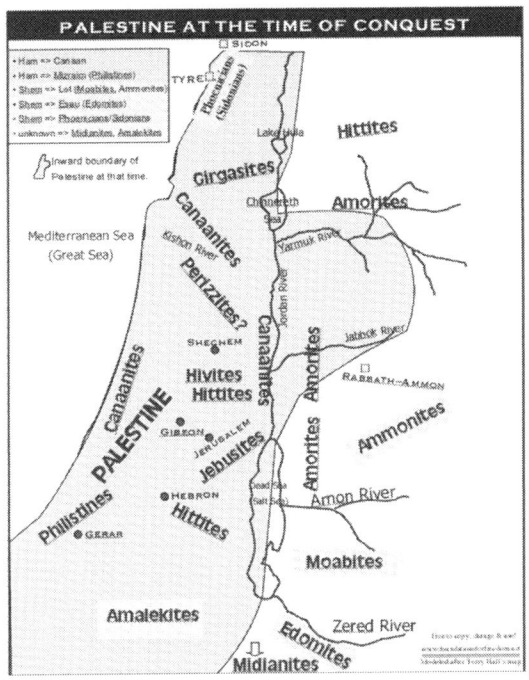

Six major people groups most influenced the biblical history of the Hebrew people: Assyria, Babylonia, Egypt, the Canaanites, Persia, and Aram (Syria). These groups, spread geographically across the Fertile Crescent, the crescent-shaped swath of agriculturally abundant land stretched from Egypt north to Syria and south through Mesopotamia.

Here is an appreciation of the cultures that were raised up by God:

The Amalekites were the descendants of Amalek, Esau's grandson. They lived in the south near Mt. Sinai, and soon after the Israelites left Egypt, the Amalekites would be their first adversary. The Israelites fought many wars with the Amalekites after they moved into Canaan. In the book of 1 Samuel, God told King Saul to destroy the Amalekites; he disobeyed, and it was only later, as recorded in 1 Chronicles, that the Amalekites were finally destroyed.

The Ammonites, descendants of Abraham's brother, Lot, lived northeast of the Dead Sea. Lot had a son named Ben-ammi, the father of the Ammonite people. The main city in the area of Ammon was Rabbah or Rabbath Ammon, after which the modern capital city of Amman, Jordan is named.

The Amorites lived near the Jordan River. In the book of Genesis, Abraham helped the Amorite king, but later, the Amorites and Israelites fought many wars. When the Israelites were traveling toward Canaan, Sihon and Og, two Amorite kings, fought bitter wars with them.

The Babylonians lived in the area that is now the country of Iraq. Abraham was born in the city of Ur in Babylonia, of which the capital was called Babylon. Babylonia is most remembered by the king named Nebuchadnezzar who attacked the Israelites, destroyed the temple in Jerusalem, and took many of the Israelites back to Babylonia in exile. In Jamaican folk culture, Babylon is the caricature of everything that is military, foreign, or representative of dominance and law.

The Canaanites, (considered by some scholars as the Phoenicians) were the merchants who traveled around the area and sold things. They were famous for purple dye, made from a special sea animal. Many Canaanites lived by the Mediterranean Sea. They also lived further to the east. The Canaanites worshiped many false gods. God warned the Israelites not to worship their false gods.

The Chaldeans also lived in the area that is now the country of Iraq.

The Girgashites were in the same group of people as the Hivites.

The Hittites originally lived in the countries that we call Turkey and Syria. They were the first people to use iron to make tools.

The Hivites means "villagers" or "midlanders". They lived in the middle of Canaan and also in the northern part of Canaan. They may have been related to the Hittites. They may also have been called "Horites".

The Jebusites lived near the city now called Jerusalem. When they lived there, they called the city Jebus.

The Midianites were the descendants of Abraham and his concubine Ketura. The Midianites lived south of Canaan in the area near Sinai. Moses' wife was a Midianite.

The Moabites lived in the area of Moab. Moab is east of Canaan. The Moabites are descendants of Lot. Lot was Abraham's brother. Lot had two sons--Moab and Ben-Ammi. Ben-Ammi was the father of the Ammonite people. Moab was the father of the Moabite people. A Moabitess (woman Moabite) in the Bible was Ruth.

The Perizzites lived in the areas in the southern and southwestern part of Canaan. Their name means "villagers". They may have lived in the open in town with no walls around them.

The Philistines are a well-known group today this date. They lived near the sea. They probably came from another place, possibly Greece. They had 5 big cities: Gaza, Ashkelon, Ashdod, Ekron, and Gath. The Philistines were skilled in iron smithing. This means that they took iron from the ground and made it into thing they used, like tools and weapons for fighting in wars. They fought many wars with the Israelites. Two of the Philistines mentioned in the Bible were Delilah and Goliath. In the book of 1 Samuel, the Philistines stole the Ark of the Covenant. God punished them, and then they returned it to the Israelites.

The Phoenicians lived in the area that is now called Lebanon. Some people who study history think the Phoenicians are the same as the Canaanites. Other people think they are different. Some of the cities of the Phoenicians were Sidon, Byblos, Tyre, and Ras Shamra. The Phoenicians were skilled with boats and ships.

Sidonians-- The Sidonians came from the city of Sidon in Phoenicia. A Sidonian who was mentioned in the Bible was Jezebel.

Surrounded by all these different nations and cultures, the distinguishing element that emerges is the inherent power that each culture maintained. It would be unfair to conclude that there was present in the Jewish people a particularity that was unique to them. The reason for the broiling antagonism that was ubiquitous among these people groups was their conviction that theirs was unique, and that they were brought into existence to be models of excellence to the other nations. Might it not be the design of God to separate people in order to strengthen them? At least this author is thoroughly convinced that there is a passion that God exhibits throughout the pages of the Holy Writ.

Later on in this book we would be developing this conviction of mine that culture trumps religion. It all began here in the Old Testament. Every nation that surrounded the people of Israel lived with the constant reminder that culture trumps religion. The sad commentary is that we tend to so spiritualize the accounts of biblical history that we are blinded to the power of the cultural interpretation of what God is about in this world. God is a culture God. God can only be understood through God's interplay with culture.

In an excellent 2010 article[27] prepared for a magazine that I published Ken Crow speaks to the issue of the dominance of culture. He states, "When Jesus became flesh and lived among us (John 1:14), it was in a particular social, historical, and cultural setting. It might have been easier to understand if God incarnate had rejected all existing cultures and somehow created a dramatically new culture separate from all others. But, he didn't. His life in a first century Jewish family changed that culture and history. And yet in most ways his life seems to have been amazingly normal. In many areas he seems to have adapted his life and ministry to the culture into which he came, while also vigorously opposing some aspects of the culture."

More to the point is the manner in which we interpret what the Bible is saying to us today. Many a local Biblical theologian has fallen off the interpreter's cliff by forgetting that this Bible that we revere is not an American book written for Americans and using American terms. Many misunderstandings come about because of the failure of people to understand things in the Bible that are cultural and unique to the societies in which the Bible had its origins. A perfect example is the use of the term *father* in genealogical sequences. If you ask me who my *father* is, I am very likely to identify one individual man. *Father* to an American is the person who was involved in conception. To the ancient Jew however, *father* was any blood relative who was a hero. In Matthew 1:1 the writer tells us "Jesus Christ, the son of David, the son of Abraham." Does this mean that Jesus was the grandson of Abraham? Just reading the rest of the chapter tells us that this is not the case. A Jew regarded *father* to be a term that indicated descendancy, but not that the person listed was actually involved in his conception.

Another cultural landmine is the manner in which the genealogies are recorded in the Gospels. Matthew's genealogy gives us 42 generations, while Luke records 55 generations. I doubt that Matthew was ignorant of Luke's sources of genealogical history. It is merely that different cultures record genealogical history differently, and the Bible honorably respects the power of cultural, rather than dispelling the nuances of any particular culture. What is important for us in the 21st century is to appreciate the power of culture throughout the Bible.

But is there purpose in this diversity in the Bible? You bet there is. Or at least, so I think. When Paul found himself confronted by the Areopagan crowd on Mar's Hill he stated, "From one man *he made every nation of men*, that they should inhabit the whole earth; and *he determined the exact places where they should live*. God did this so that men would seek him and perhaps reach out for him and find him, though he is not far from each one of us." (Acts 17:26-27). God relishes in the uniqueness of culture. Without different cultures there is no God. Because God exists, culture lives on. The psalmist captured it correctly,

For you created my inmost being;

> you knit me together in my mother's womb.

I praise you because I am fearfully and wonderfully made;

> your works are wonderful,
>
> I know that full well.

My frame was not hidden from you

> when I was made in the secret place,
>
> when I was woven together in the depths of the earth.

Your eyes saw my unformed body;

> all the days ordained for me were written in your book
>
> before one of them came to be. (Psalm 139:13-16)

CHAPTER
FOUR

JESUS – A FIRST CENTURY CULTURAL ICON

The New Testament continues this concern for history by also beginning with a genealogy. The life of the Messiah is placed in the context of Israel's history, and Jesus' lineage becomes an important part of placing His life into context. Jesus Himself refers to the chronicles of the Jewish people—He does not teach in a cultural or historical vacuum. Instead, His words are infused with historical reference and an awareness of His cultural context. In the life of the early church as revealed by the epistles, we see the importance of remembering the life and history of Jesus. The Scriptures remind God's people to reflect on what has gone before.

Jesus Christ was a cultural icon of and for the Jewish people. I would opine that it was God's providential purpose to use the Jewish people as a vehicle through which God's purposes could be accomplished. This is not to denigrate any other people group, but to demonstrate the usefulness of culture and its significance as a carrier of the salvific design.

To begin the discourse, let's take a look at the genealogies which two of the gospel writers painstakingly present within the biblical oracles. Both Matthew and Luke determined that, in order to legitimize Jesus' Jewish heritage, a tracing of his ancestral tree was necessary. (Matthew 1:1-17 and Luke 3:23-38). The culture was deemed significant.

Genealogy is a record of ancestors, or descendants. The Bible provides two of them for Jesus Christ, one by Matthew in Matthew 1:1-17 and the other by Luke in Luke 3:23-38. Although both clearly show that Jesus was descended from Abraham, Isaac, Jacob (who God renamed as *Israel*), Judah (from whose name *Jew* is derived) and King David, there are slight differences that have caused many to ask the question, "Why 2 *different* genealogies for Jesus Christ?"

Matthew's Genealogy Of Jesus Christ

Matthew's account moves *forward* in time, providing a list of descendants beginning from Abraham:

"The book of the genealogy of Jesus Christ, the son of David, the son of Abraham."

"Abraham was the father of Isaac, and Isaac the father of Jacob, and Jacob the father of Judah and his brothers, and Judah the father of Perez and Zerah by Tamar, and Perez the father of Hezron, and Hezron the father of Ram, and Ram the father of Amminadab, and Amminadab the father of Nahshon, and Nahshon the father of Salmon, and Salmon the father of Boaz by Rahab, and Boaz the father of Obed by <u>Ruth</u>, and Obed the father of Jesse, and Jesse the father of David the king."

"And David was the father of <u>Solomon</u> by the wife of Uriah, and Solomon the father of Rehoboam, and Rehoboam the father of Abijah, and Abijah the father of Asa, and Asa the father of Jehoshaphat, and Jehoshaphat the father of Joram, and Joram the father of Uzziah, and Uzziah the father of Jotham, and Jotham the father of Ahaz, and Ahaz the father of Hezekiah, and Hezekiah the father of Manasseh, and Manasseh the father of Amos, and Amos the father of Josiah, and Josiah the father of Jechoniah and his brothers, at the time of the deportation to Babylon."

"And after the deportation to Babylon: Jechoniah was the father of Shealtiel, and Shealtiel the father of Zerubbabel, and Zerubbabel the father of Abiud, and Abiud the father of Eliakim, and Eliakim the father of Azor, and Azor the father of Zadok, and Zadok the father of Achim, and Achim the father of Eliud, and Eliud the father of Eleazar, and Eleazar the father of Matthan, and Matthan the father of Jacob, and Jacob the father of Joseph the husband of Mary, of whom Jesus was born, who is called Christ."

"So all the generations from Abraham to David were fourteen generations, and from David to the deportation to Babylon fourteen generations, and from the deportation to Babylon to the Christ fourteen generations." (Matthew 1:1-17 RSV)

Luke's Genealogy Of Jesus Christ

Luke's account moves *backward* in time, providing a list of ancestors all the way to Adam, and God:

"Jesus, when He began His ministry, was about thirty years of age, being the son (as was supposed) of Joseph, the son of Heli, the son of Matthat, the son of Levi, the son of Melchi, the son of Jannai, the son of Joseph, the son of Mattathias, the son of Amos, the son of Nahum, the son of Esli, the son of Naggai, the son of Maath, the son of Mattathias, the son of Semein, the son of Josech, the son of Joda, the son of Joanan, the son of Rhesa, the son of Zerubbabel, the son of Shealtiel, the son of Neri, the son of Melchi, the son of Addi, the son of Cosam, the son of Elmadam, the son of Er, the son of Joshua, the son of Eliezer, the son of Jorim, the son of Matthat, the son of Levi, the son of Simeon, the son of Judah, the son of Joseph, the son of Jonam, the son of Eliakim, the son of Melea, the son of Menna, the son of Mattatha, the son of Nathan, the son of David, the son of Jesse, the son of Obed, the son of Boaz, the son of Sala, the son of Nahshon, the son of Amminadab, the son of Admin, the son of Arni, the son of Hezron, the son of Perez, the son of Judah, the son of Jacob, the son of Isaac, the son of Abraham, the son of Terah, the son of Nahor, the son of Serug, the son of Reu, the son of Peleg, the son of Eber, the son of Shelah, the son of Cainan, the son of Arphaxad, the son of Shem, the son of Noah, the son of Lamech, the son of Methuselah, the son of Enoch, the son of Jared, the son of Mahalaleel, the son of Cainan, the son of Enos, the son of Seth, the son of Adam, the son of God." (Luke 3:23-38 RSV)

Both Genealogies Of Joseph?

The major cause of controversy is that two seemingly different genealogies are provided for Joseph (while ignoring that none is presented for Mary). That part of the enigma actually has the likely answer. Very simply, one of the listings *is* that of Mary. Simple logic demands that Joseph couldn't have two sets of ancestors, while Mary had none.

Although there are a number of other theories, many Biblical scholars believe that Luke's listing is for Mary, and Matthew's is for Joseph.

Some then may ask, "Why include Joseph at all (apart from the fact that it was the custom to record genealogies through the father, even when he was a step-father, the reason Joseph's name was there instead of Mary's), since he was a step-father, and it was Mary that provided the actual ancestry back to King David?"

Both Joseph and Mary were descended from David. Joseph's record satisfies the *legal* requirement of primogeniture (inheritance rights, and responsibilities, usually went from the father to the oldest son, *or* legal step-son) for the line from David, while Mary's satisfies the *actual physical descent* from David. All requirements, legal and genetic, are fully met.

Whether we like to admit it or not, Jesus was a Jewish icon. His ministry functioned within the walls of Jewish tradition. In Matthew 10:5-6 we are told that Jesus sent his 12 disciples specifically not to Gentiles and Samaritans, but to Jews. Furthermore, in Matthew 15:22-28, Jesus tells a Canaanite woman asking for help that He was only sent to the Jews. God chose to establish Himself through Abraham and his descendants, the nation of Israel (Genesis 12:2-3). And, through this lineage, Jesus would be born. So, Jews were not only the chosen people, but also a blessing to all people as the lineage from which the Messiah would come.

Prophecies in the Old Testament all point to Jesus as the fulfillment of all of history as the Savior of mankind. When Jesus came, his primary purpose was to die for sins, but he also needed to start establishing his church. This was the primary purpose for the 12 apostles - they would spend 3 years with Jesus to learn from him, and to be discipled by him. The cultural identification and missiology of Jesus is important because it seems that in God's salvific design, culture trumped religion.

So, looking at this together, it appears the reasons why Jesus preached primarily to the Jews only were:

1. Jesus was the fulfillment of the promises of the Old Testament, given primarily to Jews.
2. God through history had focused His message through the Jews.
3. The Jews were the ones knowledgeable in the Old Testament and what God had done to prepare for Jesus,

so they would be the best ones to take His message out to the world.

4. God was preparing to bring His message to all mankind (Luke 24:47, Acts 1:8), but God needed to first establish a foundation. The focus on Jews was to build a stable foundation before it was taken to the Gentiles.

5. Notice this foundation was really the 12 apostles, not Jews in general. Jesus preaching really was focused on the 12 apostles.

I advance the conviction in this chapter that Jesus was a Jewish icon. Jesus was sent to the Jews. This might surprise most people… Gentile (all Non-Jews) and Jew alike, but he was the promised Messiah to God's chosen people Israel. He was the fulfillment of the Law and the prophets that they had been studying and following for centuries. Today we claim him as the Savior of the whole world. But the truth is that his ministry was very selective and targeted. Of course, there are designs of God that must be left unquestioned. Whatever the design of God might have been in perfecting the plan of salvation, this one thing is certain, Jesus was the fulfillment of the promise given through the First Testament pages. "Do not go among the Gentiles or enter any town of the Samaritans. Go rather to the lost sheep of Israel." (Mt 10:5-6)

As a matter of fact, Jesus avoided non-Jews as best he could because he was not called to minister to them during his lifetime. There are those few with faith who begged His grace, and then he granted it, but he was mainly dedicated to the task of bring the Kingdom of Heaven to the Jew who had had this promise made to them since Abraham. God's plan was to offer His Kingdom and with it the choice between eternal life and eternal judgment, first to the Jew and then to the Gentile. (Rom. 2) The Jews will all come to know their Messiah at the end times as has already begun to happen, but they had to be blinded for a time so that his grace could come to the rest of the world (Rom. 9-11).

The early Church began by Jesus, was entirely Jewish. This was who Jesus lived out his ministry for; it was only after his death that the Church began reaching out to the rest of the world.

Some salient reminders might be noteworthy:

- The Scriptures have come through the Jewish people. The Bible describes their history and their religion.
- Jewish people wrote the entire Old Testament. They wrote the entire New Testament with the possible exception of the apostle Luke.
- Jewish people preserved the Scriptures throughout history. The Jewish people protected the Bible against destruction by its enemies.
- Prophets like Ezra and Nehemiah "guaranteed" the accuracy of our existing text by their painstaking copying methods.
- Jesus came from the Jewish people. He lived as a Jew and followed Jewish religious practices, even to the degree that he refused to abolish Biblical Judaism, "Do not think that I have come to abolish the Law or the Prophets; I have not come to abolish them but to fulfill them. I tell you the truth, until heaven and earth disappear, not the smallest letter, not the least stroke of a pen, will by any means disappear from the Law until everything is accomplished.(Matthew 5:17).
- The promises of salvation are all specifically Jewish in nature, "I will surely bless you and make your descendants as numerous as the stars in the sky and as the sand on the seashore. Your descendants will take possession of the cities of their enemies, and through your offspring all nations on earth will be blessed, because you have obeyed me."(Genesis 22:17-18)
- The way of salvation is Jewish, Jesus declared, "Believe me, woman, a time is coming when you will worship the Father neither on this mountain nor in Jerusalem. You Samaritans worship what you do not know; we worship what we do know, for salvation is from the Jews." John 4:22.
- The origin and existence of the church for the first several years were due to the efforts of the 12 Jewish Apostles,

and the first missionary enterprises were as a result of a passionate loyalty to the Jewish iconoclastic figure, Jesus.

Whatever the designs of God were for the eventual inclusion of the Gentiles into the salvific plan, Jesus understood the dispensational exclusivist nature of his mission while on earth -- "A Canaanite woman from that vicinity came to him, crying out, 'Lord, Son of David, have mercy on me! My daughter is suffering terribly from demon-possession. Jesus did not answer a word. So his disciples came to him and urged him, 'Send her away, for she keeps crying out after us.' He [Jesus] answered, 'I was sent only to the lost sheep of Israel.' The woman came and knelt before him. 'Lord, help me!' she said. He [Jesus] replied 'It is not right to take the children's [Jews] bread [blessings and miracles reserved for them] and toss it to their dogs [the Canaanite, or the Philistines].' 'Yes, Lord' she said, 'but even the dogs eat the crumbs that fall from their masters' table.' Then Jesus answered, 'Woman, you have great faith! Your request is granted.' And her daughter was healed from that very hour." (Matthew 15:22-28)

The most devoted followers of Jesus were not short on proclaiming the Good News to the culturally selective. As Luke records it, "Now they which were scattered abroad upon the persecution that arose about Stephen travelled as far as Phenice, and Cyprus, and Antioch, preaching the word to none but unto the Jews only." (Luke 11:19).

I recalled that while a student at Howard University School of Divinity, students of New Testament were required to attend a Jewish temple on Saturday morning. In preparation for the visit, Professor Newheart made a succinct statement and then asked a very troubling question. First, Newheart stated that we were summoned to the temple to participate in a Jewish worship because Judaism had given a rich ecclesiastical reservoir to Christianity. There was a link between the two faiths that is often forgotten by the adherents of the latter faith. His follow up question was troubling to those who dared to answer. It was this, "What has Christianity given to Judaism, in exchange?"

No one dared to answer. My guess is that the answer would have been brutally honest, and it would have revealed a fatal flaw in the way Christianity has been practiced. Sadly, we have inserted in our practice an unhealthy division between faith and history, between the divine and the man, between worship and apologetic. Very often people are not interested in the Jesus of history, the so-called "historical Jesus" but they are content with the one they have come to worship even if the resemblance is distorted, exaggerated or quite different altogether. It could very well be that the rigid dissonance that exists between Jews and Christians today is a result of Christians' attitude of disdain and disrespect for the umbilical cord that gave birth to the Christian faith.

Some have claimed that this attitude is a result of a lack of citation of Jesus' sayings by the New Testament writers. As an example, the four gospels are bursting at the seams with facts about Jesus' ministry, yet Paul prefers to concentrate on the risen Christ and virtually ignore his human lifespan and teaching. It is no wonder that some have mischievously or skeptically claimed that Paul turned the brand of Judaism that Jesus taught into a new religion: Christianity. It could very well be that Paul, as a missionary called to ministry among non-Jews, sought to deculturize Christ so that the ministry among the Gentiles could find its rightful place. Paul made the mistake that is so often made today, that in order to legitimize one's culture one must lessen the importance of the other's. It was not necessary for Paul to lessen the importance and significance of Jesus Christ as a cultural icon with a message and ministry specifically to the Jewish people. To be culturally intelligent is to uncover this Jesus from the ecclesiastical wrappings in which he has been presented and worshipped.

The question that lingers to this day is whether Jesus ever intended to divorce himself from the Jewish culture. Did he understand the implications of his Jewishness? Did his disciples fully appreciate the import of this cultural exclusivity as God's design? Did Jesus come to set up a new religion?

As old as these questions might be, they still stir up controversy and offense. Jesus has been made out to be, not only a Western Christian, but also white, blond, blue eyed and on Hollywood's casting list. The Jewish scholar, Geza Vermes, was reprimanded by the chaplaincy at an English University for suggesting that

Jesus was a Jew.[28] American films have had the phrase, "Moses was a Hebrew, **Jesus was a Christian**". Friedrich Delitzsch (son of Franz, the evangelical scholar) said **Jesus was a Gentile.**

This reminds me of a discussion I had while being pastor of the Community of Hope in Washington, DC. Ramesh was a devout follower of Christ who had been converted from the Hindu faith. He was well versed in the Hindu religion and because of my interest in world religions, he and I spent long hours talking about the challenges Hindus face when confronted with the claims of the Christian Gospel. One of the aspects that emerged was the reverence Hindus maintained for the liberator of India, Mahatma Gandhi. Gandhi had left India when he was in his early twenties for post secondary education in colonial England, and having completed his education, was called to the bar.

As Indians migrated to South Africa, very soon there was a growing population established there. The young barrister Gandhi left England for South Africa and became the richest lawyer representing the interests of Indians in South Africa. We all know the end of the story. Gandhi liberated the Indians of South Africa from the tentacles of British rule, and then at age forty-four, returned to India to lead them in the historic non-violent, civil disobedient struggle against British rule.

What Ramesh believed, and I tend to agree with him, was that God was the unseen hand behind the liberation of India. No one else in India could have brought about such an improbable movement of the people. As a Hindu and an Indian, Gandhi was indispensable to the struggle. Gandhi was an Indian icon, like Jesus was to the Jews, to be used by God in Moses-like obedience when the time was right. Culture trumps religion, every time!

CHAPTER
FIVE

THE EARLY CHURCH CONFRONTS CULTURE

Many a sermon has been preached on the topic, "on one accord." The Pentecostal experience that captured the early church has been fodder for millions who read the narrative with somewhat clouded visions because of the sheer powerful significance of the event. It is important for us to revisit the events of the early church, for in them we find clues about the ethno challenges that plagued the organism, even threatening to destroy them, but for the Acts 15 Conference on Cultural Intelligence. If one should revisit the machinations of this early movement it would be clearly evident that they were definitely not in one accord regarding the implications of the mission mandate to take the gospel from the geographical center in Jerusalem to the ends of the known world.

Far from presenting an ideal picture, Luke, the author of Acts, revealed that the Twelve, with its decisiveness in responding to the needs of the faithful and its openness in blessing diversity in the community, were not always with one accord. The Jewishness of the group posed challenges to its authenticity from its inception, and clearly threatened to jettison its mission.

I would like to cite three incidents in the book of Acts that seem to imply that culture trumps religion, every time. They are the Pentecost outpouring of the Spirit (Acts 2), the neglect of the Hellenist widows (Acts 7), and the Jerusalem Council (Acts 15).

Without question, the greatest challenge for the nascent church arose out of the frustration of trying to find a happy medium between the long held belief that the newly found faith was God's peculiar gift to the Jewish community and the enthusiasm with which Gentiles accepted this new faith claim. The defining moment came as the disciples convened on the Day of Pentecost. The overriding theme of Pentecost could possibly be the absolute impartiality of God towards ethnicity and culture. But this very attitude of God towards impartiality has been sadly cited as a rationale for the elimination of culture, rather than an acceptance of the mandate by God to respect and appreciate the beauty and uniqueness of culture.

Prior to Pentecost, the Jews were plagued with schizophrenia about their faith. It was founded upon their interpretation of history. To them, the new faith must originate with them as the nucleus. Then occurred the phenomenon of Pentecost. Gathered on that day were not only all those who lived permanently in the capital, but those who came to Jerusalem from different places, from Parthia, Media, Elam and Mesopotamia, Cappadocia, Pontos, Asia, Phrygia and Pamphylia, Egypt and Libya, Rome, Crete, and Arabia. All these people, whether they were Israelites by birth or foreign proselytes, or were not proselytes at all but were at Jerusalem for various reasons, all this people, representatives so to speak of all the known world, heard the Apostles speaking in their own language and dialect about Jesus Christ.

Many there are who view this episode as the reversal of Babel where God seemed to have brought disunity through the introduction of varied languages. I vehemently disagree with this comparison. What we witness on the day of Pentecost was not that the disciples all spoke in one language. The real miracle of Pentecost was that each culture, each tribe, each people group heard the good news in its own language and dialect. Culture trumped religion. Much has be made of the cyclonic wind of Pentecost. But equally phenomenal is the Spirit's decision to translate what had been previously considered the language of God. No longer will the power of the mother tongue of the Jewish people be the vessel of God's authority. But now God has been liberated to use other languages. Culture won the day!

At Pentecost the Holy Spirit moved on a handful of Palestinian Jewish people who become messengers of God's good news. Just as God worked at Babel to "mix" languages so that people began to scatter, God moved at Pentecost to "mix" the languages spoken by the first followers of Jesus so that scattered people would learn what God has done in Jesus Christ to make us one people. God moves in mysterious ways, and one of those ways is the mystery of unity in diversity that always elevates one's culture rather than destroying it. Gathered on that historic day were people from many nations. Those living or dwelling there permanently were from twelve different nations, but those sojourning were there for the feast both Jewish and proselyte (converts to Judaism) from Rome; Cretans and Arabs.

They were dispersed Jewish "dwellers" (dispersed Jews who took up residence) in Jerusalem because, according to Luke 2:25 and 38, they were waiting for the Messiah to come and save Israel. These dispersed Jews who actually lived in and took residence in Jerusalem were originally born from 12 other nations and three different dispersions.

These 12 different countries represented by those actually living in Jerusalem, and they were there on the Day of Pentecost. They composed of: (1) Parthians, and (2) Medes, and (3) Elamites, (4) and those who inhabit Mesopotamia, (5) and Judaea, (6) and Cappadocia, (7) Pontus and (8) Asia, (9) Phrygia and (10) Pamphylia, (11) Egypt, (12) and the parts of Libya which is near to Cyrene.

There were also in the crowd on that day of Pentecost sojourners or visitors from Rome, Crete and Arabia who simply came to keep the Jewish feast of Pentecost, and were not necessarily awaiting the Messiah to save Israel. They were Jews and those converted to Judaism.

So, there were Jewish dwellers in Jerusalem from 12 different nations. The sojourners are simply travelers that may or may not have been born in Rome or Crete or Arabia. This accounting of the nations is significant because one must appreciate the miracle of Pentecost in the context of God's favor extended to these various cultures by granting them the blessing of the outpouring of the Holy Spirit as the fulfillment of the Joel prophecy.

I was in discussion recently about the difficulty of missionaries who are compelled to take the gospel to the ends of the earth. Language is often one of the greatest challenges. Just imagine that in Papua New Guinea there are more than 500 languages, some almost undecipherable. On this side of the ocean we have only to go to New York City where we are informed that there are also more than 500 languages spoken. Pentecost is being repeated every day around the world. The miracle of Pentecost, however, is that those present heard the disciples' message in their own language. There was no attempt by Divine fiat to use one language, but ears were touched, and culture became the interpreter of the historic message that would empower and transform this small band of coward disciples.

Pentecost validates the power and significance of culture. No attempt was made to lessen the power of culture. In fact, every culture, expressed through their individual language, became the willing hearers of the message. Culture trumps religion, every time!

The earliest Christian church was an unusually complex phenomenon. Cultural and linguistic diversity between the Hebrews and the Hellenists in the church of Jerusalem necessitated the existence of separate Christian synagogues and worship. Christians were worshipping separately from other Jews from the very beginning, even while joining them in Temple worship. Christians meeting in house churches devoted themselves to breaking of bread and prayer in two languages, Hebrew/Aramaic and Greek. Like any other organization, the early church soon found out that there are growing pains that accompany any attempt to be loyal to a mandate. Their mandate was to spread the new message of the resurrected Christ. Ananias and Sapphira emerged as the first serious threat to derail the authenticity of the movement, and judgment was swift. In their case, nothing that the disciples did was brought into question because, as Luke reports, God acted. Upon the heels of this severely punitive measure by a loving, yet apparently merciless God, was the complaint by the Grecian Jews that the Hebraic Jews were overlooking their widows in the daily apportionment of food.

Really, what was the true nature of this dispute? I have visited this narrative on many occasions, but seem to miss the cultural implications hidden within the story. Bible scholars are in steep disagreement regarding the real problem of Acts 6. No less an esteemed scholar like James Montgomery Boice suggests that the problem they faced was merely one of ineffective administration brought on by the rapid growth of the movement.[29] The New Interpreter's Bible claimed that it "was the problem of supply and demand that growth had created."[30] C. K. Barrett shrugged it off as "a minor deficiency in administration."[31]

C. Peter Wagner suggests that the true nature of the problem facing the early church was not administrative of religious in nature, but it was cultural and political. His conclusion is drawn from a closer look at the protagonists in the plot. Wagner claims that the Hebrews were more than likely, Judeans, Aramaic speaking, who had personally known Jesus, and used this acquaintance to claim a spiritually superior posture. On the other hand were the Hellenists who were not fluent with Aramaic, were Greek speaking, and had no personal reflection or memories of the historic Christ. They very easily may have succumbed to an inferiority complex.[32]

These contrasts brought upon the movement a cultural challenge that seemed insurmountable at the time. The Hebrews who spoke the Aramaic language of Jesus and were more familiar with the ceremonial laws easily could have felt superior to their Hellenists brothers and sisters who were more conversant with Greek, the lingua franca of the community. Although the two groups "were one in heart and mind" (Acts 4:32), the subtle cultural differences and nuances in the language were likely to create misunderstandings and, in such cases, the Hebrews would claim authority in clarifying them, which were often in favor of themselves knowingly and unknowingly.

In spite of the passion for the growth of this new movement, culture threatened to create a perpetual problem, unless it was recognized for what it is, a potent force to be reckoned with. I would imagine that it is not far-fetched from the truth for me to suggest that because the Hebrews were sociologically closer to the Jesus culture they developed a common bond that became exclusive. They became the power brokers in the decision-making process, and this caused undue suspicion by the Hellenists when some in their group were being neglected.

What we see here is a case of social injustice taking place, practiced by one culture upon another. The religious common denominators were obviously present, but that did not in the least militate against social injustice to rear its ugly head. Again, culture trumped religion! If those words sounded a bit harsh, let me offer a more quiet tone expressed by Wagner, "their spirituality was not deficient, their missiological sensitivities were" (1994, 142). This incident is one that should not be glossed over, especially for those of us who are involved in the multicultural church. Both the Torah and the example of Jesus mandate that the community pay special attention to helping widows. (Deuteronomy 10:18; 14:29; 16:11, 14; 24:17, 19-21; 26:12-13.) The law even specifies a curse for those who neglect the poor (Deuteronomy 27:19).

The prophets stress the responsibility of "doing justice" for widows. (Malachi 3:5; Isaiah 1:17, 23; 10:2; Jeremiah 5:28; 7:6; 23:3; Ezekiel 22:7; Psalm 93:6.) In the New Testament, the epistle of James reflects the importance of such justice, insisting that true religion includes looking after orphans and widows in their distress (1:27). Mechanisms for aiding widows had long been promoted in Judaism. Jews had developed a system of aid to the poor and those in need. Religious communities such as the Essenes had a kind of social security system that provided for members' needs. But here Christians are neglecting their own.[33] Yet, in spite of these clear pronouncements, the preferential posturing by one group over another emerged as a challenge for the church.

Acts 13 and 14 describe the first missionary journey of Paul and Barnabas, beginning and ending in Antioch. While Paul and Barnabas made it a point when they entered a city to preach the Word to the Jews first, they also ministered specifically to the Gentiles; and many Gentiles believed as a result of their preaching.

There was no difference in the Gospel that Paul preached to the Jews and to the Gentiles. His message in Acts 13:16 - 41 gives us a snapshot of what he was teaching. He emphasized the death and resurrection of Jesus, the Messiah, then pointed out briefly the significance of Christ's resurrection to those who believed on him. As is recorded, "Be it known unto you therefore, men [and] brethren, that through this man is preached unto you the forgiveness of sins: And by him all that believe are justified from all things, from which ye could not be justified by the Law of Moses" (Acts 13:38 – 39). No difference in the message was necessary for Jew or Gentile. The Gentile who believed would be saved. The Jew who refused to believe would perish. What was significant was that he was preaching salvation to the Gentiles without requiring them to become Jews first. Paul and Barnabas were very open about their reasons for doing so, as in their reply to some Jews who objected to their preaching the Gospel to Gentiles:

"Then Paul and Barnabas waxed bold, and said, 'It was necessary that the Word of God should first have been spoken to you: but seeing ye put it from you, and judge yourselves unworthy of everlasting life, lo, we turn to the Gentiles.

For so hath the Lord commanded us, [saying], 'I have set thee to be a light of the Gentiles, that thou shouldest be for salvation unto the ends of the earth'." Acts 13:46 - 47.

When Paul and Barnabas returned to Antioch, they reported to the church there that "God... had opened the door of faith unto the Gentiles" (Acts 14:27). After this, they stayed with the believers there for a "long time" (Acts 14:28) without controversy. Clearly, the saints in Antioch had no problem with Gentiles accepting Christ as Lord without first becoming Jews, even though this was clearly something new to them.

The problem began when some saints from Judaea (not necessarily from Jerusalem) came to Antioch and taught that one could not be born again without first becoming a Jew.

"And certain men which came down from Judaea taught the brethren, [and said], 'Except ye be circumcised after the manner of Moses, ye cannot be saved.' When therefore Paul and Barnabas had no small dissent and disputation with them, they determined that Paul and Barnabas, and certain other of them, should go up to Jerusalem unto the apostles and elders about this question" (Acts 15:1-2.)

The historical background of prejudice in Acts 15 resulted in a resistance to the changes occurring during the time of the Jerusalem Council. In Acts 15:1 and 5, we are told that the Judaizers "came down from Judea to Antioch and were teaching the brothers: 'Unless you are circumcised, according to the custom taught by Moses, you cannot be saved.' ... Then some of the believers who belonged to the party of the Pharisees stood up and said, 'The Gentiles must be circumcised and required to obey the law of Moses.'" The Judaizers were insistent on the Gentile believers becoming circumcised as Jews before becoming Christians. In this way, the Jews would maintain the numerical majority and, therefore, the political and social power in the church. This was a cultural war going on. It is probably safe to inject here that the driving force behind the need for the Jerusalem Council was the fear of losing power. The Jewish believers wanted to set the standards for the early church and therefore insisted on the maintaining of power through the setting of the standards.

On further examination, the plot thickens because there seems to be precedent. Since the time of the Israelites' exodus from Egypt, fellowship with God and access to the promises of God were pretty much limited to Israel, "the Circumcision". Even Jesus Christ, during his ministry, limited his work to "the lost sheep of the house of Israel" (Matthew 15:24), and forbade those who he sent out to preach among the Gentiles (Matthew 10:5-6). The Gentiles received only "the crumbs which fall from their masters' table" (Matthew 15:26-27). A Gentile could gain access to the promises of God only by becoming a proselyte. For a man, that meant that he had to be circumcised.

In the book of Acts, chapter fifteen, we find one of the most significant events that took place in the early church, the Jerusalem Council, which was approximately twenty years after Pentecost. The supernatural events, such as miracles or displays of God's power, often attracts the headlines and the attention, but the Jerusalem Council, though not flamboyant, displays the providence of God working through the dedicated and consecrated leaders of the early church. Historians recognize that there have been seven ecumenical councils in the first several centuries of the early church, but the first and most significant council was the Jerusalem Council, for it answered the most momentous doctrinal question of all: What must a person do to be saved?[34]

The problem that needed to be addressed is introduced to us in the first five verses of the fifteenth chapter of Acts. The specific problem is mentioned in verse one, "And certain men which came down from Judaea taught the brethren, and said, Except ye be circumcised after the manner of Moses, ye cannot be saved." Again, in verse five the dilemma is mentioned, "But there rose up certain of the sect of the Pharisees which believed, saying, that it was needful to circumcise them, and to command them to keep the law of Moses."

Cultural preferences again threatened the early church. To some, the grace of God was insufficient to accomplish the salvific dimensions of Calvary; the new initiates to the faith must keep certain aspects of the Mosaic code. Known as Judaizers, this group was adamant in their conviction that grace was insufficient. The problem here was that these Judaizers could not accept the notion that this new cultural group could become

Christians without first becoming obedient to the old code, even to the degree that they be circumcised.

It is well known that Paul and Barnabas argued vehemently against such practice, declaring that the ritual of circumcision was not necessary to salvation. As a result of the disagreement, Paul and Barnabas went to Jerusalem, the mother church, to discuss the situation with the apostles and elders. Warren Wiersbe, teaches that the Jerusalem Conference was made up of four different strategic meetings. The first was a public welcome of Paul and his associates (Acts 15:4), then there was a private meeting that involved Paul and the key leaders of the church (Galatians 2:2). The next meeting was a public gathering where the Judaizers and Pharisees presented their case (Acts 15:5, 6, Galatians 2:3-5) and the last meeting is recorded for us in Acts 15:6-34.[35] Peter smashes the conference with a statement that defined the mode that God chose to employ in the act of salvation, "And put no difference between us and them, purifying their hearts by faith." Notice Peter said, "by faith," not "by keeping the Law." The last thing that Peter said was that by constraining the Gentiles to keep the Law, it would be a yoke upon the neck of the disciples. This is the same idea that Jesus shared in Matthew 23:4, "For they bind heavy burdens and grievous to be borne, and lay them on men's shoulders; but they themselves will not move them with one of their fingers."

What was in play here was the duel between religion and culture. No passion for the new theology of missions was sufficient to escape such a situation to explode into the Jerusalem Council. The theme for this conference could easily have been "Does Culture trump Religion?"

From the beginning Christians had inherited the Jewish social consciousness -- the belief that they were "the people of God" in the fullest sense of the words. As St. Clement of Rome wrote, "Behold the Lord taketh to himself a nation from the midst of the nations, as a man taketh the first fruits of his threshing floor" (I Clement XXIX. Therefore in order to understand the basis for the need of the Jerusalem Council, we must first reflect on the community life of the primitive Church, and the institutions by which it was maintained.

Especially important, from this point of view, are the ancient rites of Christian initiation and the institution of the catechumenate, the lengthy preparatory stage through which converts had to pass before becoming full members of the Church. As I mentioned in other places, submission to the Mosaic laws and obedience to the outdated rites was the fulcrum that maintained the old Jewish culture. The leaders found it difficult to separate themselves from that culture. After much discussion, Peter got up and addressed them: "Brothers, you know that some time ago God made a choice among you that the Gentiles might hear from my lips the message of the gospel and believe. God, who knows the heart, showed that he accepted them by giving the Holy Spirit to them, just as he did to us. He made no distinction between us and them, for he purified their hearts by faith. Now then, why do you try to test God by putting on the necks of the disciples a yoke that neither we nor our fathers have been able to bear? No! We believe it is through the grace of our Lord Jesus that we are saved, just as they are. Peter asserted that we are all saved by grace and that there is nothing distinctive about us that merits God's love.

Therefore, there is a unity and a commonality in our salvation experience. James, the leader of the pious Jews, demonstrated real strength of character in his response, even though he had much to lose in this confrontation. He, as others did, wanted to keep the faith pure and would seek to maintain power in order to maintain that purity. In verses 13–8, he demonstrates that he had not completely lost sight of God's heart for the lost in lieu of racial purity. Instead, James turns to Scripture to determine his perspective. When they finished, James spoke up: "Brothers, listen to me. Simon has described to us how God at first showed his concern by taking from the Gentiles a people for himself. The words of the prophets are in agreement with this, as it is written: 'after this I will return and rebuild David's fallen tent. It's ruins I will rebuild, and I will restore it that the rest of mankind might seek the Lord, even the Gentiles who bear my name'."

CHAPTER
SIX

THE HOMOGENOUS UNIT PRINCIPLE

As a missionary to India, Donald A. McGavran (1897-1990) became absorbed with the cause of the dirth of conversions over a fifty year period, despite a mammoth investment of resources and personnel. No statement in the church growth movement has had a greater impact on the methodology of evangelism in the twentieth century than that of Dr. Donald McGavran that "people like to become Christians without crossing racial, linguistic or class barriers." This concept was called the Homogeneous Unit Principle (HUP), and was later fully developed and propagated by McGavran's student, C. Peter Wagner. According to Wagner, an HU could be defined as a section of society in which all the members have some characteristic in common.

The abiding question for McGavran was "How do peoples become Christians?" His emphasis was on the plural "peoples." He wanted to understand the dynamics that were in play when groups of people were confronted with the claims of the Gospel. At one point he states the question thus: "How, in a manner true to the Bible can a Christward movement be established in some caste, tribe or clan which will, over a period of years, so bring groups of its related families to Christian Faith that the whole people is Christianized in a few decades?"[36] McGavran's approach to the dilemma was couched peculiarly in his concern with ethnic identities, his assumption that the question could be answered with sociological research, and an honest quest for a correlation between inputs and outputs.

His conclusion was that "Among those who think corporately only a rebel would strike out alone, without consultation and without companions. The individual does not think of himself as a self sufficient unit, but as a part of the group. His business deals, his children's marriages, his personal problems, or the difficulties he has with his wife are properly settled by group thinking. People become Christian as this group-mind is brought into a life-giving relationship to Jesus as Lord."[37] This conclusion became the core element in the HUP argument.

The HUP, strongly defended by some and unfairly criticized by others, must be understood in the context through which it was birthed. McGavran had studied the growth pattern (or lack thereof) of his own missionary movement during the fifty year period in India and other places.

The issue is accentuated by modern life. Traditionally a congregation was defined by two things that they held in common – the gospel and their locality. But many urban people live in dormitory suburbs in which they do little more than sleep. There is little sense of neighborhood. Community is defined in other ways – overlapping communities of work, family, leisure and shared interest. If community and geography are diverging which road should the church follow? If the community of people with whom I work is more significant to me that the community among whom I live, why not have a church of my work place? If community is defined by common interest rather than common location then why not interest-group churches? And where do the limits lie? If I can be part of a virtual community on the internet then why not be part of a virtual internet church? Or should we develop 'matrix churches' in which neighborhood expressions of church co-exist with other expressions of Christian community. Could I belong to a workplace 'church' and a local church?

That is, the barriers to the acceptance of the gospel are often more sociological than theological; people reject the gospel not because they think it is false but because it strikes them as alien. They imagine that in order to become Christians they must renounce their own culture, lose their own identity, and betray their own people.

Advocates for the HUP argue that there are primarily two reasons why the HUP held the potential for effectiveness as a strategy for reaching individuals with the Gospel. First, it was the strategy used by Jesus. The passion that Jesus bore for fallen humanity trumped the religious protocols of the day. He began his ministry with a very targeted and inclusive group of people called the Israelites, as he ate, drank, preached, and lived like an Israelite. When the time came to select the disciples Jesus limited himself to one homogeneous group. There was no Gentile, Samaritan, Idumean, or Hellenistic Jew. Either Jesus could be considered a segregationist, or that he was a missiological strategist. Secondly, as Peter has so often argued, missionary success in India, Taiwan, Mexico, and Denver are vivid examples of the power of the HUP.

Before entering into more detail of the HUP I must confess that, contrary to many today who seem to vilify the HUP as a strategy that is passé and dispensationalist, I strongly believe that the HUP is grounded in sociological principles rather than theological themes. The HUP does not retard congregational integration, but simply expresses an observation that is descriptive before it is prescriptive.

People groups (a term that I prefer to use rather than HU) must be accepted as creations of God. They are targets of evangelistic efforts because we have been commissioned to reach the world with the Gospel. The challenge before us is to honestly embrace a people group, warts and all, with the conviction that because God is engaged in the uniqueness of the group, evangelism cannot be reduced to cultural imperialism by one group. To level all cultures into a colourless uniformity is a denial of the Creator and a disrespect of God's creation. The preservation of cultural diversity honours God, respects man, enriches life, and stimulates evangelization. Each church, if it is to be truly indigenous, should be rooted in the soil of its local culture. The richness of every culture should be preserved, not destroyed, by the Gospel. Francis Dubose, who coined the word *missional*, wrote that God is a sending God. We are a sent people. The very fact that we are a sent people implies that there is a possibility that there might be a target for evangelism. The HUP simply reinforces the truism that culture trumps religion, and that targeting a people group for evangelism might just by the most pragmatic approach to accomplishing our goals.

Theologically, Wagner defends the HUP principle through what he calls a "harvest principle." The unquestioned principle of farming is that of the harvest. The farmer's goal is to gather in a crop of whatever he planted. Wagner goes so far as to cite Jesus' parable of the sower whose seeds fell into four places. We need to be reminded that only one of the four places was a fruitful location for the seed. The seed that fell on good ground produced fruit in great quantities. The "soil," according to this interpretation, is "people who have been so prepared that they hear the word and understand it." From this, Wagner concludes that effective strategies of evangelism attempt to identify the most receptive people. Practically speaking, Wagner supports this principle by pointing to various areas of the world that are clearly more receptive to the gospel than others, such as Africa,

Asia, and Latin America.[38] Similarly, people groups could be viewed by their receptivity as a cultural enclave.

True, as with every other strategy, there are blind spots in the HUP experiment. If care is not taken, the HUP will be found guilty of promoting segregated churches, and the process of evangelism would be maligned and found to be archaic. In fact, Wagner was heard to opine that "If strenuous evangelism means to multiply homogeneous churches, multiply them . . . The evangelistic mandate is more important than the cultural mandate." Every church growth movement has had its areas of concern, for one cannot expect to apply the basic principles of such, without first contextualizing it to a particular situation.

Another blind spot in the HUP is the possibility of being too lenient about the unpalatable or unacceptable elements within a people group. This challenge was dealt with at the Lausanne Conference of Theology and Education Group from May 31 to June 2, 1977, in Pasadena, California. Several conclusions were arrived at that seemed to adequately address the dangers of the excessive use of the HUP. If, when approaching culture repentance is underemphasized, it would be paramount to what Bonheoffer called "cheap grace;" and if it is overemphasized, we would be guilty of preaching the law rather than grace. Furthermore, if "sin" is not clearly identified and denounced we are asking for repentance in a vacuum; on the contrary, if we overemphasize the sin problem we arrogantly usurp the convicting work of the Holy Spirit. A healthy balance must be prayerfully sought so that culture might become the agent of transformation through tolerance and wisdom.

Many have accused the HUP of being segregationist. This is indeed sad, considering the contribution that ethnic-specific churches have made to the evangelism successes of many evangelical denominations. One cannot have the proverbial cake, and eat it too! In my years at the headquarters of my denomination I have had to vigorously defend the sponsoring of the National Black Conference, an event that brought more than 1,500 Black Nazarenes together. To my Caucasian colleagues they often accused such an event as being separatist, but nothing could be further from the truth.

For many years the Hispanics have convened under the auspices of well-intended initiatives like evangelism or education. Other groups like the Haitians and Koreans have similarly convened, without being maligned. For obvious reasons, a Black Conference didn't carry the same justification as other language-specific groups did simply because many made the mistake to equate culture with language. Culture is not language, and language is merely a contributory factor in the formation of culture. As with the motivation behind the HUP, the Black Conference was a means towards an end, which is to celebrate what God is accustomed to implementing within cultures. Culture trumps religion, and it will forever by the pragmatic approach to embrace a methodology that facilitates the reaching the culture for the Christian cause.

If the HUP is to reclaim its rightful place as the most effective means of reaching people groups, it must be defended on the grounds that its strength is to be found in its capacity to enable the church to fulfill its mission of evangelism, a task it cannot abdicate.

Another criticism of the homogenous unit principle is that it denies the reconciling nature of the gospel and the church. It weakens the demands of Christian discipleship and it leaves the church susceptible to partiality in ethnic or social conflict. It has been said that "the homogenous unit principles is fine in practice, but not in theory." The fact remains that most congregations are homogenous to some extent. People choose congregations on the basis of cultural affinity, worship-style, denominational loyalty, theological prominence and even cultural background. As soon as one chooses to operate in one language a homogeneous group has been created.

So the question should be posed, should we then establish groups or plant churches that target those otherwise marginalized by our churches? Or does this maintain the failure to take seriously the reconciling nature of the cross that was the problem in the first place? Should we work harder at reconciliation and establish churches that reflect heterogeneous cultures and sub-cultures? Wrong! The answers to these questions are incomplete because they are not contextual on the surface. The faux pas emerges because we fail to distinguish mission and ministry. Such a shortcoming could be mitigated by three postulates:

1. Homogeneity is a principle of mission while reconciliation is a principle of ministry. Homogeneous groups are effective when they are in the context of mission, but as people are converted and discipled they must be encouraged to work towards reconciliation by becoming advocates for intra-congregational intermingling.

2. The congregations of the Early Church may have been systems of household churches. It is possible that these household churches were fairly homogeneous. Nevertheless, the reconciling nature of the gospel found expression in the city-wide identity of these household churches. This structure allowed the apostolic churches to express both homogeneity and cross-cultural and ethnic reconciliation. McGavran and Wagner says: "The biblical teaching is plain that in Christ two peoples become one. Christian Jews and Gentiles become one new people of God, part of the one body of Christ. But the one body is complex. Since both peoples continue to speak separate languages, does not the oneness cover a vast and continuing diversity."

3. Planting churches targeted at marginalized groups is legitimate in order to prevent that social marginalization being cultivated within the church. If there were a 'level playing field' the socially dominant culture would also dominate in the church.

We are all agreed that the dividing wall, which Jesus Christ abolished by his death, was *echthra,* "enmity" or "hostility." All forms of hatred, scorn, and disrespect between Christians of different backgrounds are forbidden, being totally incompatible with Christ's reconciling work. But we must go further than this. The wall dividing Jew from Gentile was not only their active reciprocal hatred; it was also their racial and religious alienation symbolized by "the law of commandments and ordinances." This, too, Jesus abolished, in order to "create in himself one new man in place of two, so making peace" (Eph. 2:15).

This did not mean that Jews ceased to be Jews, or Gentiles to be Gentiles. It did mean, however, that their racial differences were no barrier to their fellowship, for through their union with Jesus Christ both groups were now "joint heirs, joint members of the same body and joint partakers of the promise" (Eph. 3:6 literally). The union of Jews and Gentiles in Christ was the "mystery" which was revealed to Paul and which he proclaimed to all (Ephesians 3:3-6, 9, 10). Thus the church as the single new humanity or God's new society is central to the gospel. Our responsibility is both to preach it and to exhibit it before the watching world.

What did this mean in practice in the early church? It seems probable that, although there were mixed Jewish-Gentile congregations, there were also homogeneous Jewish congregations (who still observed Jewish customs) and homogeneous Gentile congregations (who observed no Jewish customs). Nevertheless, Paul clearly taught them that they belonged to each other in Christ, that they must welcome one another as Christ had welcomed them (compare Romans 15:7), and that they must respect one another's consciences, and not offend one another. He publicly rebuked Peter in Antioch for withdrawing from table fellowship with Gentile believers, and argued that his action was a denial of the truth of the gospel, that is, of the justification of all believers (whether Jews or Gentiles) by grace through faith (compare Galatians 2:11-16). This incident and teaching should be taken as a warning to all of us of the seriousness of permitting any kind of apartheid in the Christian fellowship. And it should go without saying that no one visiting a church or requesting membership in it should ever be turned away on merely cultural grounds. On the contrary, visitors and members should be welcomed from all cultures.

Dr. Bill Sullivan, who for many years gave leadership to the US – Canada Region in the Church of the Nazarene, is well known for engineering a shift in the church growth movement. Prior to his elevation as director, the starting of new churches was relegated to districts and District Advisory Boards. After many years of negative growth patterns, Bill threw a bombshell into the church growth initiatives. His conviction to his dying days was that the most effective way for the Nazarene clan to sustain a modicum of church growth is for churches to start churches.

This shift opened the doors unwittingly to the many people groups who were making America home. Greater meaning was given to Sullivan's discoveries and pronouncement when, in 1997, the Board of General Superintendents declared that the United States and Canada are the new mission fields. What this did for the church growth movement in the denomination was the concentration of evangelism and church planting among people groups. Church planting took on the task of reaching out to the people groups through the use of the HUP, though not explicitly stated. Sullivan brought to the department a young minister who had ministered in the urban centers of Washington, DC, Tom Nees. It was Nees who singlehandedly emphasized the need to reach the new mission fields through the implementation of Ethnic Strategy Committees representing the various groups of immigrants, and this emphasis resulted in a harvest of souls and the starting of congregations among different peoples.

Today, while growth among the Caucasian Nazarene population has not kept pace with the general population growth, ethnic representation and evangelism among these groups has been admirable. In 2012 there were more than 550 Hispanic congregations, 142 Black congregations, 75 Korean churches, 87 Haitian churches, and more that 50 churches for the First Nations Peoples. In addition, there are 17 other people groups that have been evangelized. These encouraging signs have all resulted from the recognition that peoples and willing to embrace new religious affirmations without crossing racial and ethnic lines. The words of McGavran will come alive again, "If God's plan for the salvation of the world is to be carried out, a mighty multiplication of living congregations must occur in most pieces of the mosaic in most countries. Through it multitudes of men and women will find peace, joy, and power in the forgiveness of their sins and assurance of salvation. And because of the large numbers of citizens who will then be living and voting, serving and ruling as dedicated followers of the Lord Jesus, tremendous increase in individual and corporate righteousness will become possible. Churches are the most potent instruments of social advance known. They must be multiplied in every piece of the marvelous mosaic. That is the challenge of church growth."[39]

A few years ago the Church of the Nazarene adopted a new statement of mission – "To make Christlike disciples in the nations." While it is true that conversion is an individual act, one must not lose sight of the implications of the statement for world evangelism. People groups can come to God. People groups can decide that the Christian faith holds more promise for them than their present faith does.

In Matthew 28:19 Christ instructs Christians to disciple the peoples (ethne). In Hindi, the national language of India, the words read *sab jatiyan ko chela karo*, that is, "disciple the castes"- a much more accurate rendering of the Greek than the common English version, "make disciples of the nations." What our Lord said was precisely "disciple the tribes," the castes and families of the earth. Just as the Jewish tribes were the people of God, so the multitudinous peoples of the Gentiles should become God's household. Understanding that culture trumps religion, it makes perfect sense to target populations of people for mass evangelism.

The first ten chapters of Acts make numerous mentions of multitudes becoming Christian. In the New Testament we repeatedly come upon the conversion of households - *oikoi* in Greek. The *oikos* pattern, once seen, is a noteworthy feature of New Testament church growth. The by-product of the oikos pattern has been the introduction of targeting.

Prior to the HUP initiative, missionary efforts seldom kept records of growth, or for that matter, neither were they acquainted with line graphs nor did they make numerical projections. Wagner lamented that "they set goals for their business activities, the number of cars they will sell, the amount of steel they will produce, or the number of new buildings they will erect; but not for the number of converts their church will win." With the advent of the HUP, this new practice of setting numerical goals was adopted. Of course, the conditions under which most missionaries labored made it unwise to set goals. They became preoccupied with maintenance rather than mission. It became therefore popular for missionaries to say "As far as members are concerned, let us take what God brings to us, love them and rear them as good Christians. Let us teach them the Bible, habituate them to weekly worship, and train indigenous leaders for them. The tithe must be taught, congregations organized, problems of the new churches solved, and Christians made into good Christians. We must establish a form of Christianity that fits the existing economic level, and the dominant culture. While some noxious elements of the culture (such as idol worship) must be purged, most elements can be brought into the church, which will increasingly take on a thoroughly indigenous hue. The task is not setting membership goals but laboriously and lovingly forming the kind of Christian community that is thoroughly Christian and that feels thoroughly at home in its culture."[40]

The historic turning point came in 1971 when the Evangelical Committee on Latin America commissioned Peter Wagner, Virgil Gerber, and Edward Murphy to a consultation in Venezuela. The theme of this conference seemed to be the benefits of targeting and keeping records of evangelistic conversions among people groups. Forty-seven pastors met in 1972 and the Church Growth Bulletin in November 1973 published this report:

"Spanish-speaking pastors of ordinary churches brought records (some woefully inadequate) of their membership during the past ten years. Workshop leaders taught them how to analyze, chart, and understand the growth which had taken place and was taking place. That provided a background of reality. The pastors were talking about their own problems, tasks and opportunities. They were not reacting against new North American schemes! In that setting it became fruitful to set forth church growth principles-they could then be seen as "something we need." The third step was to ask the participants, on the basis of their past experience (in faith and after prayer), to project the growth they believed God was calling on them to attempt. The fourth step was to calculate what the average rates of growth during the last ten years had been, and during the coming five years would be. The last step was to plan for another workshop a year later, attended by these same men, to see what in fact had happened. The Venezuelan experience furnished a base for a significant advance in church multiplying evangelism. Dr. Gerber prepared a small book, A Manual For Evangelism/Church Growth, which told how any group of pastors and/or missionaries could hold a church growth workshop." (McGavran 1973:368).[41]

Thus started, thanks to the HUP, an aggressive accounting of the efforts of missionaries worldwide. Needless to say, most of this accounting was in cross-cultural ministry where people groups were the targets.

Across the United States and Canada church growth seminars flourished. Denominations caught fire. The Church of the Nazarene was a beneficiary of this new currency: "The Church of the Nazarene, which began in 1906[8], had grown very vigorously in the early years but started slowing down in the fifties. By 1970, with a membership of 600,000, it showed signs of plateauing. In 1974, it threw itself into the recovery of growth. Its national leaders called meetings of all pastors. Raymond Hurn, then head of the Home Mission Board and now a general superintendent, committed his board to planting many new churches and allocated personnel and money to that goal. It created a Department of Church Growth and appointed Bill Sullivan as director."[42]

No doubt, evangelism throughout the world will continue to be on the upswing. It will forever be clouded by those who advocate for an all inclusive sowing of the seed, and that's a good thing if we are to be obedient to the mandate of the Gospel. However, the most significant growth would take place when homogenous groups are targeted by intentional strategies by denominations and mission boards. We will forever owe a debt of gratitude to the passionate advocates of the HUP who were committed to selective evangelism and at the same time recognizing that the claims of the Gospel are to reach *panta ta ethne*, all the disparate groups with the Gospel. Culture trumps religion, every time.

CHAPTER SEVEN

THE 5-5-5 MISSIONAL STRATEGY FOR STARTING ETHNIC SPECIFIC CHURCHES

Introduction:

The 5-5-5 Missional Plan is offered as a helpful challenge to Nazarene denominational US & Canada "mission directors and coordinators" to strategizing church growth based upon three targeted initiatives. They include the challenge to:

1. Identify and foster **five potential new "ethnic" or cultural leaders** who could be challenged to plant new Nazarene ministries.
2. Identify and nurture **five effective sponsoring churches**, both suburban and urban.
3. Identify and enlist the support of **five key district superintendents** who could strategize, with the director and co-ordinator, new and viable ministry in five new populations or communities.

Below are suggested actions that merit further discussion, tweaking, and expansion:

Implementing the 5-5-5- plan

I. Identify and foster five potential new "ethnic" or cultural leaders who could be challenged to plant new Nazarene ministries.

According to one Biblical scholar, Jesus spent 50% of his waking time mentoring the inner core of leadership among the disciples. They were Andrew and Simon Peter, James and John. They did not come to him as part of a church package of leadership. He went into the world, identified them, already noting their natural leadership abilities, called them, and spent a great deal of time, not only instructing, but showing them what the mission was about. As part of their training, he then sent them out with clear instructions as to how to conduct themselves in a hostile world. When they failed, he didn't "rail" them, but used their failures as teaching moments.

Here is a suggested sequence to identify and foster five potential new leaders of your "ethnic" responsibility who could be challenged to plant new Nazarene ministries.

1. **Seek God's Direction:** Pray regularly and consistently that the Lord will give you workers for "the harvest."
2. **Study the Need and Opportunity:** Research and read over the denominational materials that describe demographic details about the population group to which you are especially assigned. These can be found at www.nazareneresearch.org.
3. **Survey Potential Personnel:** To identify potential ethnic leaders, look to the following sources:

    - Nazarenes who attend majority group congregations.
    - Nazarenes who attend non-majority congregations.
    - Students studying in our Nazarene colleges.
    - Newly-transposed Nazarene leaders from your cultural homeland.
    - Former Nazarene missionaries well informed or experienced in your culture, or referrals from these individuals.
    - Individuals from other denominations who show authentic interest in potentially becoming Nazarene ministers.
    - Referrals from the Global Ministry Center, regional directors, district headquarters, and local pastors.
    - Other like-minded denominations who can't find placement for their "ethnic" leaders.
    - Referrals from current credible "ethnic" pastors.

1. **Screen Potential Candidates:** Make an initial contact to see if the target person has any interest at all in pursuing some level of ministry at this time or later. Indicate that you are seeking a one-year relationship to a small group of leaders and that the timing and circumstances may

not be conducive to a "special" relationship currently. *Make no promises.*

2. **Scrunch the Information:** Create an informational template that records the names of these candidates including: past personal history, past and present ministry history, formal ministerial credentials, Nazarene involvement---past and present, current assignments (both sacred and secular), family and legal status, academic ministerial training, personal issues, ministry gifts and graces, motivational issues, "red flag" cautions.

3. **Scale the Names:** Rank potential candidates on overall suitability, timeliness, and availability, prioritizing several who might engage in personal mentorship.

4. **Survey the Opportunities:** Is there a potential match between the best candidates and the imagined opportunities for ministry?

5. **Select the Best:** Present a plan to those given highest priority that includes your personal commitment, a staged series of mutual commitments, and benefits.

6. **Secure a Covenantal Commitment:** This should be mutually agreed on by both the mentor and the mentored in ministry. It should include a practical time-frame for the relationship, a listing of the commitments and benefits of the relationship and a means of terminating it, if it doesn't work.

7. **Specify the Terms of the Covenant:** There should be a negotiated formal agreement between you and the prospective minister.

   For the prospective minister, the Covenant should specify:

   - A commitment to becoming Nazarene.
   - A commitment to preparing for formal Nazarene ministry service.
   - A commitment to regular engagement in being mentored.

- A commitment to rectify "deficiencies" in ministerial training, and in personal or legal issues.
- A commitment to practice where possible, ministerial gifts.

For the mentor, the Covenant should specify:

- The length of the special relationship.
- The frequency and nature of contacts.
- A negotiated plan for training and exposure for Nazarene service that include issues of attitude, knowledge, and skills necessary for both Christian and Nazarene service.
- Advocacy for ministry opportunities.
- Resourcing with readings, conferences, district activities, etc.
- Honest feedback.
- A gracious means of backing out of the covenant on either side.
- **Share the Joy:** The opportunity of specialized ministry to particular "ethnic" or cultural groups engages both risk and satisfaction. The mentor needs to promote new leadership, tell the story of emerging leaders as broadly as possible, clarify and enlist resources to make the process more convenient, and find settings of ministry conducive to the gifts and cultural relevance of the new leaders.
- **Sanctify the Relationship:** See it as a "set-apart" relationship surrounded with prayer, counsel, and purpose towards the end of utilizing the calling, gifting, and graces of the emerging leader for impacting the people group that you represent. If it doesn't mature into a ministry assignment, view it still as ministry to the individual, to the family, and

eventually, to the community. Identify an on-site supervisor/mentor to take the relationship on beyond even your commitment.

II. Identify and nurture five effective sponsoring churches, both suburban and urban.

Jerusalem had been devastated. Yet according to the book of Nehemiah, God's vision was that it should be repopulated and restored to the witness and glory that God had intended for his Holy City. It was left to the exiles (those outside) and the remnant (those inside) under the leadership of Nehemiah to enter into a partnership to help restore the city. Nehemiah mobilized resources from outside including a "tithe" of the exiles (11:1-2) to appropriate and relocate in Jerusalem, as well as organizing the locals into "community development."

Immigrants and newer populations have traditionally settled in the poorer areas of our cities. But they need the infusion of "sponsorship" partners to enter into their cultural worlds with appropriate "start-up" resources and nurturing encouragement that will jump-start situations in new evangelistic efforts within their populations. Directors and coordinators can be the "Nehemiahs" who motivate local churches to care practically for new ministry initiatives.

Here is a suggested sequence to identify and nurture five potential new effective sponsoring churches which could be challenged to plant new Nazarene ministries that represent the target ethnic, cultural, or linguistic populations that you represent:

1. **Pinpoint "Ethnic" Population Centers:** Study the latest demographics found at www.nazareneresearch.org or www.census.gov.us along with appropriate research about your particular "ethnic" or cultural calling. What issues stand out? Is yours a historical immigrant group, a new one, or a group constantly being replenished? What has been the success of the evangelical witness among this group? What have been the barriers?

2. **Profile Potential Sponsoring Congregations:** Look first to Nazarene churches who have ministry in the general area, or who have some affinity with the ethnic or cultural

group being targeted. Is there a "hang-up" or problem that may discount this ministry from engagement?

3. **Prepare Persuasive Documentation:** Go first to the District Superintendent to obtain permission to approach potential pastors and congregations. Be well armed with demographic information, with some historical and contemporary knowledge of a potential target community, its flow of immigration, its receptivity to the Gospel, its cost of doing business in that community, along with a list of potential leaders to initiate the project. Get his/her permission to engage in conversation with the local targeted pastor.

4. **Prioritize from among the Churches studied:** Select five churches of highest priority and availability to sponsor a new ethnic, linguistic, or cultural ministry that represents your target group. Learn all you can about these churches, their motivations, and their leadership team.

5. **Present a Well-Organized Challenge:** Armed with good data and a quality presentation, approach the senior pastor first, then staff and lay leaders as the pastor sets up opportunity to share your vision and passion for collaborating with this prioritized church in developing a ministry.

6. **Pray for Guidance with and for these local Church Leaders:** After a time of gestation and discussion, encourage the pastor and people to pray for God's guidance into entering into the commitment to sponsor a new ministry or congregation.

7. **Produce a Mutual List of Commitments:** Once the church has indicated its interest in sponsoring a new ministry or congregation, sit down with the pastor and people and discuss what the nature of the commitments ought to be. These commitments could include:

    - Identifying a core of committed local leaders who will take on tasks and responsibilities for seeing the vision realized.
    - Identifying and assessing the necessary resources (personnel, venue, legal, financial, etc.) that sponsorship would entail.

- Determining the time frame that the sponsorship would last and the means of slowly handing over responsibility to the emergent ministry
- Setting up a means to resolve conflicts and manage commitments.
- Determining an exit strategy if the sponsorship turns out not to be functional.

1. **Partner with the Local Church to offer Ongoing Guidance:** As director/coordinator it will be important to work intimately with the sponsoring local church to help them understand their role, responsibilities, reasonable expectations, and resources needed and offered. Keep in regular touch and offer encouragement and guidance as requested.

2. **Prepare Indigenous Leaders:** Together with the sponsoring ministry, assist "called" leaders to understand what it means to be "Nazarene." Work with the sponsor to provide theological and ecclesiastical training on how to operate within the "Nazarene culture". Seek to be a "cultural broker" between the sponsor and the leader of the new ministry.

3. **Penetrate the Target Community:** Using existing networks, other churches, organizations, and associations, saturate the cultural group with an awareness of the existence of the ministry and what it plans to service, in terms of the culture's felt needs.

4. **Pioneer New and Creative Ways of Doing Contextualized Ministry:** Help the sponsoring church to understand that the new ministry will not be a "clone" of their ministry but will use different methods of evangelism, different ways of worship, and different foci around culturally sensitive community needs.

5. **Profile and Praise the Ministry and Sponsors to Others:** Keep the denomination informed through the District Superintendent and Mission Strategy Office. Write good news articles for publication, highlighting not only the ministry being created but also the ministry that has chosen

to adopt it. Present the leaders from both sides to the District Assembly.

III. ***Identify and enlist the support of five key district superintendents who, in partnership, could strategize with the director and coordinator, new and viable ministry in FIVe new populations or communities.***

Abraham had been promised expanded land and family as numerous as the stars in the sky. However, more practically, he needed the support and blessing of jurisdictional leaders such as Melchizedek, the priest of the Lord, to fulfill God's promises in his life (Gen 14). In offering appropriate respect, along with the accountability of tithes (Heb 7:4), Abraham, in turn, received from Melchizedek, symbol of Christ and head of what would become Jerusalem, his blessing along with "bread and wine."

The District Superintendent within the Church of the Nazarene administrative structure is the duly elected leader responsible for church development within his/her area of jurisdiction. Like Melchizedek, s/he is the "gate-keeper" for all ministry initiatives in her/his geographical area. And, like the relationship between Abraham and Melchizedek, it is important that there be meaningful "exchanges" between the District Superintendent and the directors/coordinators that include accountability, resources, blessings, guidance, trust, and appropriate permissions.

Here is a suggested sequence to identify and work with five District Superintendents who are significant to the development of your "ethnic," cultural, or linguistic responsibilities:

1. **Recognize which District Superintendents currently work with your target populations.** Introduce yourself and express your interest in working closely with him or her in salvaging current ministries in crisis, strengthening other ministries, and starting new ministries. Share your resume, your strengths and gifting, your passion, your insights into the particular group where you have responsibility. If there is a district coordinator of your particular focus, develop a rapport and trust with this person, and determine how you might need to work with him or her.

2. **Rank the Five District Superintendents of Particular Focus.** Check with the Nazarene Multicultural office in Lenexa, to get guidance so that your choices are coordinated with that of the other 20+ multicultural directors/coordinators. There is the danger that too many ethnic leaders will approach the same five District Superintendents. Some of those District Superintendents that most need your attention are those with lesser experience cross-culturally and can be most positively influenced by your input.

3. **Report on the Existing Ministries on the District Superintendent's District:** Become informed about the various target ministries already in existence on the district. Provide an honest assessment of present realities along with ideas for future development of these congregations. Admit any problem areas that are real or potential.

4. **Relate Ways in Which These Congregations can be District-recognized:** One common complaint is that many of these congregations exist "under the radar" in part because of the linguistic issues. Suggest ways in which these congregations can be fully integrated into the whole district structure.

5. **Raise District Consciousness about Existing and New Works:** Become an advocate for your people group, suggesting their needs, their cultural history, their idiosyncrasies, their immigrant streams, their religious affiliations and openness, and future possibilities for ministry.

6. **Reconcile Internal Issues in Local Congregations.** Do this only with district permission and perhaps with district-assigned coordinators. Often there are conflicts between host and guest congregations that can benefit from "outside" intervention and conflict resolution. Your role as "cultural broker" could provide clarity on the issues along with appropriate healing.

7. **Refer any Unresolved Issues to the District Administration:** Any unresolved issues ultimately will fall into the hands of the district. Your insight and participation in seeking

conflict-resolution can be helpful in the decision-making process at the district level.

8. **Represent Those who Would Otherwise Have No Voice:** Often, because of issues of shame, embarrassment or fear, minority congregations are unwilling to express their real feelings. Tactful, honest, and sensitive communication to appropriate district leaders could salvage ministries from greater tensions down the road.

9. **Recommend New Ministry Initiatives:** Get permission from the district office to meet with your representative pastors to learn about their dreams for expansion or new initiatives. Present your own vision of what could be an overall vision for ministry among your people group on this district.

10. **Resolve to Plant New Ministries:** Along with your strategy "team," which should include the District Superintendent, his/her designated multicultural coordinator, or person assigned by the district to develop ministries in your people group, along with your "group" leaders, and potential sponsoring congregations, establish goals, strategies, location, resource commitments, time-lines, and personnel. You could be most helpful in identifying potential leaders for new ministries from your contact throughout the denomination.

11. **Rally the Support Forces:** Serve as a cheerleader, promoting the best of what is happening in your target ministry. Offer enthusiasm and excitement about the possibilities of ministry expansion to your people group. Enlist them as part of the strategy of church growth in all dimensions.

12. **Revitalize the "Majority" Church through Your People Group:** Don't see your ministry as exclusively to your assigned culture. Your group is a gift to the whole. Eventually many from your group will integrate into the larger American population and need to see themselves as "pilgrims" in transition, not losing their cultural "gifting" but enhancing the whole because of it. Remember that God has a special love for the "stranger" and "alien" in our midst, and so that God should radiate out to others who perhaps have become inured or oblivious to it

through their privileged position. As your group has been missionized, it now needs to witness God's love to a new culture of the pre-churched who predominate in modern day US and Canada.

NEWSTART CHECKLIST*

Checklist 1

- ❑ We have an increasing awareness that God is leading us in this work.
- ❑ A growing number of believers are regularly praying about this opportunity.
- ❑ Confirmation is growing from our church's lay leadership and pastor.
- ❑ Our primary motivation is reaching new people for Christ.
- ❑ In building Christ's kingdom, we believe the needed resources will be provided.

Checklist 2

- ❑ A free demographic study of the target area has been ordered from the Research Center.
- ❑ A profile has been designed of the people we hope the new church will reach.
- ❑ A study of existing churches of the area shows the potential of a new church (existing church population compared to community population).
- ❑ We have contacts in the target area to begin a core group.
- ❑ Our congregation has interested workers to assist this new church in getting started.
- ❑ Our congregation has completed the attached survey to determine where our members and leaders are on this opportunity.

Checklist 3

- ❑ We recognize this new church may be different from our church in its style, philosophy, and ministry methods.
- ❑ We will be willing to release control of this new church and allow its leaders to follow God's calling for their ministry.
- ❑ We will regularly conduct a "faith check" to determine our willingness to move ahead without having all the details of our questions answered.
- ❑ We will celebrate the significant milestones for this new church and rejoice in their victories to encourage and enable their future development.
- ❑ A budget is prepared that outlines our financial support for this new church.

Checklist 4

- ❑ We are in full agreement for the choice of pastor for this new church and have the approval of our District Superintendent for the pastor and targeted area.
- ❑ Our church leaders are willing to establish an interim task force for starting this church until the new church can recruit its own leadership.
- ❑ Preliminary work is being done to locate potential meeting places for the new church to begin worship services.
- ❑ Possible methods and tools for announcing the opening of this new church are being discussed and evaluated.
- ❑ The pastor of this new church is able to clearly describe his vision for starting this congregation.

Checklist 5

- ❑ An overall timeline is completed that places these checklist items on a one to three-year calendar for planning and budgeting purposes.
- ❑ The timeline allows for the new church's funding to follow at least two years behind the growth in attendance.

- ❏ The timeline permits nine to twelve months of preparation time before actually launching the new church into public worship services.
- ❏ The timeline reflects the high attendance times of spring and fall, by planning for the launch and regular outreach efforts in those seasons.
- ❏ Regular meetings of the taskforce with the starting pastor are scheduled for encouragement and accountability.

CHAPTER
EIGHT

A MISSIONAL BREAKTHROUGH – THE IMMIGRANT CHURCH

The Immigrant Churches: Toward A Stranger's Theology

Dr. Sam Vassel & Professor Gabriel Salguero

Give me your tired, your poor, your huddled masses yearning to breathe free,

the wretched refuse of your teeming shore. Send these, the homeless,

tempest-tost to me, I lift my lamp beside the golden door!

-- Emma Lazarus

Philosophy is afflicted, from its childhood, with an insurmountable allergy: a horror for the other which remains the other.

-- Emmanuel Levinas

Why A Stranger Theology?

We may be asked, why write on the immigrant church? The United States experience by and large, except for the obvious case of the Native Americans, is an experiment in immigration. Everyone, in some way, whether by force, coercion, or choice is part of the immigrant realities. Immigration is not a new phenomenon. Every generation has established some form of immigrant church. Before 1890, the U.S. witnessed the emergence of Protestant Puritans, Dutch Reformed, Irish Catholics, German Lutherans, and Swiss Mennonites just to name a few.[43] Since the turn of the 20th Century, U.S. immigration has included Asians, Africans, Latin Americans, Caribbeans, and increasing numbers of Eastern Europeans. In short, immigration continues to be a major topic in the collective consciousness of the U.S., (and we would argue the world in light of globalization), and its impact should not be ignored. Why write about the immigrant church? Simply put, the immigrant church is who we have been and who we are. Pastor and urbanologist Manuel Ortiz articulates this reality clearly:

The world is in a state of movement, responding to what demographers call push-pull factors, and it is making its mark on America . . . In 1985 Time magazine entitled an issue " ' The Changing Face of America': How Long Will It Be Before the Third World Overwhelms the First World?" In 1990 there appeared an issue entitled "What WILL the U.S. Be Like When Whites Are No Longer the Majority?"[44]

As if the history of the Church in the U.S. were not reason enough, Scripture concludes that God is the immigrants' God. The God of Abraham, Isaac, Jacob, Sarah, Rachael, and Rebekah is the God of the sojourner. Even before the divine mandate for Abram to leave Ur of the Chaldeans (Gen. 12), God had been a God of the nomads. Afterwards, in the Exodus and Exile, YHWH was continually on the move with Israel. Jesus is a stranger in Egypt. In Jesus' earthly ministry, the Markan witness shows him always on the go. The Pentecost event begins with people from every nation living in Jerusalem (Acts 2:5). Later, the Petrine epistle is addressed to the exiles in five regions of Asia Minor (I Pet 1:1). God has always been the God of the sojourner, exile, and immigrant.

Churches of all stripes have struggled toward an ecclesiology and missiology that would be welcoming to new waves of immigrants. Simultaneously, newly founded immigrant congregations have wrestled with how to "do church" in a strange land. The Psalms of the Israelites in captivity articulate this struggle, "How could we sing the Lord's song in a strange land?" (Psalm 137:4). Every generation of worshipers must ask two important questions: what can we learn from the immigrant church? What has the immigrant church learned from its relocation in a different context?

A fruitful dialogue that has implications for both long-standing congregations and hundreds of immigrant churches has begun and should continue. Our stories are only two of many and cannot encompass the complexity and nuance of all immigrant congregations. Still, the hope is that sufficient insights can be drawn for the building of the Kingdom of God. This kingdom establishes ties that bind between the immigrant congregations and their sister churches in the "dominant culture."

We believe in the power of story. Our Master was a storyteller who changed the world. We share the stories of a first-generation Jamaican pastor in the Bronx, New York and a second-generation Puerto Rican from the Jersey shore. Our stories are shared in hopes of transformation. Although our narratives vary, there are overlapping markers, which may provide clues toward a more healthy and inclusive global Church. We begin by describing the waves of immigration that have arrived at our respective congregations. After unearthing the layers of arrivals, we share what this has meant for our congregations in terms of re-examining our way of doing church. We hope that in our sharing we open the doors to a chorus of witnesses that will broaden and deepen the Christian faith in our time and place.

These two stories have something to teach. In a world where the Church is often an afterthought, the Church's lessons can "bring the weight of unjust societies, politics, and spiritual practices tumbling down."[45] A tale from two ever-changing immigrant congregations is our invitation for you to travel with us as we seek to understand the *Zeitgeist*, the Spirit of God moving through history. Our changes have led us to underline some conclusions about the DNA of the immigrant church. Whether in Lakewood, New Jersey or the Bronx, New York immigration has brought its promises and challenges. The tale of two churches is taking a close look at a small segment of the immigrant church and asking God to make us like the children of Issachar, "understanding of the times, knowing what Israel ought to do (1 Chronicles 12:32)."

A Tale of Two Churches

Imagine visiting a Spanish-speaking congregation that is mostly Cuban and Puerto Rican. Moreover, the assembly includes a small group of African-American congregants and a handful of other congregants from diverse parts of Latin America. If you can imagine this, you have just stepped into the church of my youth. From January 1979 until August 2005 I attended the Spanish Pentecostal Church. The changing face of the church community in those 26 years is the initial point of entry into this larger conversation. We, like many immigrant churches around the world, were experiencing first-hand how migration impacts the way we do ministry.

It is in my home congregation where I learned to *caminar con Jesús*.46 When my parents began their pastoral ministry the membership was predominantly Cuban and Puerto Rican, with a smaller contingency of English speaking members from a variety of ethnic backgrounds. Many of the Cubans arrived directly from Cuba or via Spain after leaving during the Cuban Revolution of 1959. Some of the Cuban immigrants were well educated, although not all. On the other hand, the majority of Puerto Ricans that arrived during the Great Migration of 1946-1964 worked in manual labor, particularly manufacturing. Cubans were considered immigrants because they were required passports. Conversely, Puerto Ricans were citizens even if the U.S. culture was totally foreign to them. Even the initial founding members of the congregation were radically different in education, citizenship-status, and socio-economic standing. Sociologist, Joan Moore, adequately describes the immigration patterns of this founding group at the Spanish Pentecostal Church:

> The major surge in Puerto Rican migration to the mainland U.S. came earlier—shortly after World War II—in the Great Migration of 1946-1964. The population has been characterized as a "restless" movement of people back and forth from the island, with a steady accretion on the mainland population. The flood of Cuban migration started, of course, when Fidel Castro took power in 1959. Successive waves of refugees almost quintupled the number of Cubans, although recently the overall rate of growth decelerated.47

Since the late 1980s and early 1990s there has been a steady influx of immigrants from all over Mexico, Guatemala, and El Salvador. The harsh economic and political crises of these countries translated into large numbers of immigrants. Both documented and undocumented immigrants arrived in Texas, California, and New York. These were not the only places they planted roots. Many came to Arizona, North Carolina, and New Jersey. This new wave of immigrants represented yet a new economic reality. Many of these immigrants worked in agriculture or as day laborers in construction, as nannies, and child-care providers. The church now had two classes of Latinos in their midst: a middle-class upwardly mobile group and a group that was struggling to survive economically. This is often the case. As one wave of immigrants meets with economic opportunity, the new wave is economically disadvantaged.

Since the early 1990s, we are no longer the Spanish Pentecostal Church but rather the Missionary Pentecostal Church. A change in the congregation's name is a manifestation of the change in local demographics.[48] The children of the Cuban and Puerto Rican members have grown up in a wider culture that was Anglo-dominant. In addition, there are several more Italian and African-American families who have become members. English was the only language an increasing number of parishioners spoke.

About 60 miles north of this Jersey Shore church at 971 E. 227th Street in the Bronx is the Bronx Bethany Church of the Nazarene. In the early 1960s, a small group of West Indian immigrants initiated this congregation. Regrettably, this group was not welcomed as part of a prominent white Manhattan church in the 1960s. Frustrated attempts to find a locale for worship led them to gather initially in their homes. After 4 years, in 1964 under the leadership of Dr. V. Seymour Cole and 21 charter members, they organized and affiliated with the Church of the Nazarene. In the 42 years since its inception, the congregation has grown to almost 700 members.[49] This growth is a classic case of how immigration impacts a congregation. The nature of the growth at Bronx Bethany is worth examining as a template for understanding immigration patterns and their impact on institutions, particularly the Church.

Nevertheless, considering this predominantly Jamaican congregation a monolith is to misunderstand the realities of immigration. Throughout the four decades of its existence, Bronx Bethany has received different waves of immigrants from the West Indies. Each immigrant group brought with it different expectations and a different understanding of their culture. Having left Jamaica at different times in its history, they all left a different Jamaica. In addition, immigrants from diverse parts of the Caribbean were attracted to this fellowship. Their arrival made a significant impact on the DNA of the congregation. The memories of the parishioners' homeland reflect what they expect from the Jamaican immigrant church in the U.S. What this has meant for Bronx Bethany is a careful nuance of how to "do ministry." This is doing ministry to a congregation of different generations of immigrants who define their culture in radically different ways.

First, there is the Jamaican gentleman and lady who left Jamaica in the late 1950s and early 1960s and have fresh recollections of the British influence in the West Indies. A new wave of nationalists emerged at the forefront of politics and culture after Jamaica left the Federation of the West Indies in the 1960s. The sway of such weighty figures as Alexander Bustamante and Norman Manley impacted the ideology of Jamaicans both in and outside the church. Bronx Bethany in addition to receiving some of the earlier group was now receiving a generation of Jamaican nationalists. Moreover, some of the children of the earlier group were U.S.-born Jamaicans. Decades later, the emergence of the neo-nationalists in Jamaica and a search for cultural renewal produced yet a different wave of worshipping immigrants at East 227th Street. These neo-nationalists often followed the thought of Michael Manley and other socialist's ideologies. Recently, the arrival of many Jamaicans who grew up in the post-Cold War reality has added yet another layer to this complex milieu.

The mosaic at Bronx Bethany is a microcosm of what is happening in immigrant churches all over the world. The colonized, nationalists, and neo-nationalists Jamaican realities are coupled with a generation of U.S.-born Jamaican all with different understandings of how to do church. In addition, in early 2006 the congregation in recognition of the large Latino influence in the Bronx launched a Latino ministry. English speaking immigrants reached out to Spanish speaking immigrants.

As the years went by, the neighborhoods changed and so did these congregations. The changing context of the Missionary Pentecostal Church and Bronx Bethany required some reinterpreting of identity and mission. Our radical demographic shifts were in part a realization of the eschatological foresight pronounced in Revelation 7:9, "After this I looked and there before me was a great multitude that no one could count, from every nation, tribe, people, and language, standing before the throne." The motley crew that was gathering together at these congregations had very different expectations of what "church" should be. The challenges and promise of worship, proclamation, leadership, and fellowship abound at both Bronx Bethany and the Missionary Pentecostal Church.

The milieu is even more complex. U.S.-born Jamaicans and Latinos who are now adults are dating and marrying across cultures. The church must not only be inclusive of the different epochs of migration but the burgeoning group of second-generation congregants. This group like any other second-generation group deals with what black sociologist W.E.B Dubois called a "double-consciousness": they are both Jamaican and American or Latino/a and American.[50] Perhaps even a triple consciousness black, Jamaican/Latino/a, and American. Immigration continues to mean adaptation to these realities. Immigration requires transformation. If we want to be inclusive of the other immigrant groups that join, the church we need to change with the times.

The Pluralistic Immigrant Church (Promises and Challenges)

One thing is clear: immigrant churches are not the representation of a homogeneity or monolith. There are waves of immigration. Each wave brings a different set of people with different expectations. There is an eclectic dimension even within each wave of immigration. If you visit a Latino or a Jamaican immigrant congregation, expect diversity. This diversity is representative of the time in which each group migrated. Not only is the immigrant church heterogeneous in terms of culture but also ideologically. The successive generation of immigrants and their children are formed by diverse worldviews. The post-Cold War immigrant and the pre-Cold War immigrant have different formative experiences that contribute to this ideological montage.

Pluralism poses both promises and challenges for leadership, worship, and proclamation. For instance, how does one provide an amalgamation of leadership that is representative of the congregation? Pluralism is not just diversity in the pews but also in leadership and proclamation. This is not an easy task, and it requires much compromise from all groups involved. Still, the investment in being a sign of the Kingdom is worth the effort. We do things because they are right, not because they work.

After 36 years of Dr. Cole's leadership, the Bronx Bethany Church recruited a new pastor. The fact that they brought in Jamaican-born Dr. Samuel Vassel as pastor shows that the ties to Jamaica remained very strong. Still, this new pastor was intentional in including U.S. born men and women on the pastoral staff. In addition, the worship at Bronx Bethany combines high liturgy that appeals to the first wave of immigrants with contemporary worship that includes Caribbean and American styles. Preaching is not just the use of the Queen's English but the *patois* can be heard from time to time, so as to honor the *lingua franca* of many parishioners. The influence of African-American preaching and worship is also being included particularly among the younger generation. Contemporary Christian singers Kirk Franklin and Fred Hammond are not unknown. New forms of leadership, worship, and proclamation are reflections of the different streams flowing into Bronx Bethany.

At the Missionary Pentecostal Church, the leadership of Pastors Héctor and Raquel Salguero had challenges akin to Bronx Bethany. The Salgueros incorporated a new multi-ethnic leadership that included an African-American woman pastor, an Italian-American trustee, and a worship team led by second generation worship leaders. The worship was a symphony of salsa, merengue, and contemporary worship music in both Spanish and English. All sermons were simultaneously translated and a project to have all songs written in both languages if possible was initiated. Today, MPC is a blend of Latino/a and non-Latino worship and leadership. While the senior leadership at Bronx Bethany and MPC remains first generation émigrés, windows of opportunities have been opened for the succeeding generations to assume these positions in the near future. Signs of change continue to emerge.

The Providing Immigrant Church

What then is the promise of the immigrant churches? The immigrant churches provide not only a spiritual haven but also a social and ethical response to minority groups that "live and work under a dominant church and society."[51] Christian ethicist, Eldin Villafañe, borrowing from Orlando Costas, writes of several identifiers that make Hispanic Pentecostal congregations a gift for the immigrant. These gifts are also true of immigrant churches across denominations, geographical regions, and language. Villafañe's taxonomy is a helpful tool for understanding how immigrant churches serve to ease the transition from a known culture to a foreign one. We will highlight four of the seven social roles Villafañe underlines as indispensable tools the immigrant church provides:

- Survival ("A Place of Cultural Survival"): "... It helps preserve or to reconstruct the value systems, language, music, art, costumes, symbols, and myths of its respective communities."
- Signpost ("A Signpost of Protest and Resistance") "...a disturbing sign on the fringes of an unjust society... a prophetic indictment against the racism, political oppression, economic exploitation and social marginalization..."
- Seedbed for Community Leaders ("Emerging Leaders ... Nurtured")
- Social Service Provider ("Natural Support Systems—Source of Strength")[52]

Cultural Survival:

How is the immigrant church a place for survival? The immigrant church is the postmodern manifestation of the synagogue. The immigrant church provides what the synagogue did for the exilic community. It brings the community together. Where else but in the synagogue could we ask questions and hear one another without fear of being labeled strange? Many who come to these congregations seek continuity to their lives and culture in a new context. The worship style is a critical component to this transition. Singing in their native tongue and preaching with a familiar cadence makes this transition much easier. Cultural survival is no small matter for the immigrant who experiences anomie and alienation in a dominant culture that misunderstands him/her and is often suspicious of his/her customs and language. During the hours of corporate worship and fellowship there is the validation and appreciation of the home culture and all that it offers. For those limited hours on Sunday or in the middle of the week, we are not singing in a strange land but at home.

Social Service Provider:

The immigrant church takes seriously that YHWH is often referred to as Jireh, the provider. Not only is the congregation providing a space for grace that seeks to overcome cultural shock and anomie, the congregation is also a social-service provider. At both the Missionary Pentecostal Church and Bronx Bethany many congregants sought the churches help with connecting to sources to facilitate the transition of new arrivals. The members who have been in the United States for some time have established a network and relationships that facilitate the transition into a new and often hostile context. New church members are connected with these networks via church relationships or at times pastoral intervention. It is not uncommon for the pastor or one of the deacons of our congregations to translate for new members at the immigration or introduce them to the social service offices in our neighborhoods.

The benevolent fund offerings, which were often used for new immigrant arrivals who were not prepared for the cold winters of the Northeast, are clear evidence of this social service commitment. Although limited economic resources often challenge the immigrant church, it pools its reserves together to provide initial sustenance for the newest arrivals. The challenge of resources fosters a creativity and camaraderie that is a marker of our location in life. Silver and gold we do not have much of but, what we do have, we give generously (Acts 3:6). It is no wonder that Dr. Cole and Rev. Salguero were both bi-vocational for the first decade of their ministries as they nurtured their congregations' fiscal health. The analogy of the widow of Zarephath is continuously repeated in the life of the émigré. We give to Elijah and the jug of oil does not run dry (1 Kings 17:14).

Indigenous Leadership:

The provision the immigrant church fosters is not just cultural survival and social service but also the gift of developing indigenous leadership. The immigrant church is the seedbed for leadership. The Missionary Pentecostal Church and Bronx Bethany have a strong history of cultivating leadership. The classical examples of Richard Griffiths (Associate Pastor for Youth), and Althea Taylor (Associate Pastor for Community Outreach), at Bronx

Bethany and Angel González and Jeanie Wilson at Missionary Pentecostal Church are just a few of the many that could be highlighted. Within the confines of a culture that respects and fosters their talents, these men and women were able to thrive. The safety provided them in a non-hostile environment as educators, preachers, and indigenous leaders prepared them well to navigate the often difficult terrain of the dominant culture. Anecdotal evidence is the children's ministry at MPC. Resident grandmother and sage, Olga Sanchez, ensured a legacy of leadership for years to come.

Richard and Althea are not just local leaders in the congregation but leaders in their District and community. The empowerment they received and the opportunities to both succeed and fail within the confines of a nurturing community released them to do the same in a more diverse context. Althea's M.Div. from Howard University, and Richard's leadership in Nazarene Youth International, have a direct corollary to a supportive community that gave legitimacy to their cultural expression of the Christian faith. Angel and Jeanie's success as an international evangelist and educator respectively are a natural outgrowth of a congregation that allowed them to take leadership roles within a smaller and non-threatening immigrant church. Many ethnic-minority global leaders of denominations and para-church organizations today were fostered in the incubator of small immigrant churches. This incubator is so successful because it not only protects but empowers generations to be who they are and impact God's Kingdom.

The Prophetic versus Parochial Immigrant Church:

Prophetic Mission:

The immigrant Church also serves as an embodiment of what Walter Bruegemann calls *The Prophetic Imagination*. His hypothesis holds true as one of its identity markers. The task of prophetic ministry is to nurture, nourish, and evoke a consciousness and perception alternative to the consciousness and perception to the dominant culture around us.[53]Villafañe points out that the church on the margins can be a prophetic indictment against all manner of oppression and marginalization. In the worship and proclamation themes of the Exodus and Exile abound. Within this theme, there is a denunciation of all the oppression that is antithetical to the liberating Gospel of Christ and an annunciation of a Gospel that makes us all free and equal. The immigrant church is like John the Baptist, *ego vox clamantis in deserto*,54 proclaiming that not everything in the dominant culture is consistent with the liberating Gospel of Jesus Christ.

As strangers, the immigrant church is uniquely situated to provide insights about the culture that insiders may miss. The opportunity for the larger church to glean from a different set of eyes is a blessing that should not be overlooked. Indeed, the immigrant church is often heard paraphrasing Elisha's prayer, "O Lord, open the eyes of the church so they may see what we see (2 Kings 6:17)." The perspective of the outsider brings a certain perspicacity and insight that could lead the church to a more comprehensive understanding of God's purposes in the world.

In what ways is the immigrant church prophetic? It resists cultural imperialisms and decries any homogenization that collapses the Gospel into the assumptions of the dominant culture. The poor among us see the downside of a merciless capitalism that can have avarice as its basic grounding and *modus operandi*. Moreover, the collective experiences of colonialism or neo-colonialism brought over from immigrant homelands is a hermeneutical lens that is watching guard over abuses of power in society and the church. The deep wounds of economic dependency, colonialism, and brutal puppet regimes places this group in a place to loudly echo the now famous maxim of Lord Acton, "Power tends to corrupt; absolute power corrupts absolutely." Walter Wink's challenge to the church to name, unmask, and engage the powers[55] is particularly evident among those of us in the exile. Prophesy, for us, is speaking truth to power and challenging the savage inequalities of power that are still prevalent in our day.

Parochial Mission:

If the immigrant church provides unique giftings to the entire body of Christ, it also faces unique challenges. The immigrant church does not in every case serve as a prophetic alternative. Conversely, it at times serves as a conclave that stifles its own growth. The area of its greatest strength is also one of its greatest challenges. Its particularity could be a strength-weakness. Conclave is from the Latin – *con* (with) –*clave* (key), literally to be locked in with a key. While this may stir up feelings of security and protection for a group in transition, it simultaneously can rouse feelings of isolationism by those outside the community. The implications for evangelism to succeeding generations and the dominant culture are great.

The challenge to the immigrant church (perhaps even more so to the dominant culture) is not patriotism but a nationalism that could lead to ethnocentrism. It is critical to discern the difference between healthy patriotism and nationalistic or ethnocentric idolatry. Patriotism is love of *patria* – (homeland, motherland, fatherland). Patriotism is the spark for a genuine love and celebration of one's formative communities and culture. God honors celebration of one's home. We must be careful also to note that some forms of nationalism are a reaction to centuries of bitter and cruel colonization that sought to obliterate a national identity. In this case it is a nationalism birthed out of what Paul Tillich called *The Courage to Be*.[56]

Still, there exists a dysfunctional nationalism equivalent to the sin of idolatry that declares God prefers one nation to others, one people over others, or one language over others. Dysfunctional nationalism rises from a very myopic theology of nations that says, "God bless us and nobody else." The immigrant church, while celebrating and honoring its distinctives, should be sure that it has understood itself as one out of the multiple cultural manifestations of the multiform grace of God. *E Pluribus Unum* is not just a slogan or motif but an experiential reality we proclaim daily.

Beyond Parochial Mission:

The Jonah paradigm is here most noticeable.[57] "And the word of the Lord came to Jonah, son of Amathia, and he said, "Go to the capital of Iraq (Ninevah is the capital of Iraq), and preach against it. Go to the capital of Iraq and tell them I have an opportunity for them. I'm giving them a second chance." But consider that Jonah had suffered from an Assyrian trauma. The Assyrians, when they took people, cut their ears off, so they would never hear again. They plucked their eyes out, so they would never see again. And they cut their tongues out, so they would never worship again. Jonah's hatred was a serious one. He was the colonized, and they were the colonizers. It is like evangelizing the very center of the people who have treated you wrongly and overcoming your hatred.

Jonah's mission is a decolonizing text in which the oppressed becomes the messenger. Jonah is mission from below. Mission from below overcomes the missiological challenge. It is the immigrant church saying, "We cannot overpower you and say you must listen so we'll do it another way." It is that great paradox for mission that is a prophetic-servanthood (not to be misread as slave) always challenging, transforming, and redeeming. This is not a colonial mission but a post-colonial mission that resists suppressing and eradicating everything it encounters. Colonial mission was too often "patronizing, condescending and mentally enslaving."[58] This mission from below is a gift that seeks to redeem the roots of Christian evangelism from the many centuries of European colonization. Mission from below finds its hope in the Biblical witness that began from the underside in a militarily occupied Jerusalem and changed the uttermost parts of the earth.

This does not mean that there is no place for the monolingual first-generation immigrant congregation. Rather, this first-generation congregation must allow for other manifestations of second and third generation children to establish new methods of ministry for their time and place. No single type of immigrant church will minister to the entire immigrant reality. There are multiple methodologies that can be employed: a) a homogenous, monolingual congregation made-up of mostly first generation immigrants, b) a heterogeneous congregation with one worship service that is inclusive of all styles and preferences (a monumental pragmatic challenge), c) a congregation with multiple worship services and programs and one intentionally-diverse governance, d) multiple congregations sharing the same space with distinct governance.

Toward A Stranger's Theology (Initial Steps)

Although a project that highlights the full theological and missional significance of the immigrant church is beyond the scope of these initial musings, we are simply outlining some initial steps, which may lead to a more fully developed stranger's theology. We must ask and re-ask the fundamental query: what role does the stranger play in God's economy? We are inviting the global church to a prolonged conversation that will seek to establish what Eric H.F. Law calls, "The Peaceable Realm."[59] This preliminary cartography is the aperture to an extended commitment to a more mature articulation of the *intellectus fidei* concerning God and the stranger.

The immigrant church is Christological declaration. We are the hybrid, mestizo, and multicultural church that understands experientially the incarnation. The incarnation is Jesus navigating his divine-human hybridity: he is both fully God and fully human. The immigrant Church understands that we often have to live in the in-betweeness of being American and being "other."[60] We are always neither/nor and not both/and to those who do not understand the complexities of living in both worlds. We challenge both the Gnostic or Docetist's heresies that say you must be only one, the present manifestations of these heresies writ large is the homogenizing of the church without respect to its diversity. We celebrate Christ's incarnation and hybridity because it models for the Church what it ought to be living in and with the people while celebrating oneself.

This church is a theological-anthropological statement. It boldly declares that we are all *imago-Dei*. Since we as a people gathered from all over the earth are created in the image of God, we have worth and dignity. Our worth is not predicated on our place of birth, our native tongue, or our economic status. Imago-Dei says that God's imprint on humans is what gives them their worth independent of the color of their skin or on which side of any border they were born. Imago-Dei proclaims that God's image is reflected in multiple colors, languages, and cultures.

The immigrant church is an embodiment of the Trinitarian creed. Our God is a relational God. God's internal relationship is the model for the church. In the words of the classic hymn, "God in three persons, blessed trinity." The immigrant church declares that we don't have to be one person to be one. In our ontological differences, our very personhood is not merged but rather accepted as co-equal. The life of the immigrant Church allows us to be Trinitarian not just in our creed but also in our deeds.

This church is a pnuematological confession. We believe that the Spirit that gathered all the regions of Asia Minor at Pentecost for the benefit of global mission is blowing still. The Holy Spirit is not subject to cultural preferences and a Social Darwinism that privileges one group over another. The Spirit allows us all to hear in our own language so that the Kingdom may be established. The Spirit challenges biases and parochialisms while celebrating culture and language. The pnuematological impulse of the church is that we are all immigrants led by the Spirit's power and wisdom.

The immigrant church is an eschatological sign. In its paradox of respecting and resisting culture, it demonstrates God's intent to work through and in life without being subsumed by it. In this sense, the mission of the immigrant church shares the impetus of pre-colonial evangelism that had the potential to engage pagan culture to empty it of its demonic meaning and to reload its symbols with the redemptive message of the Christian faith. Samuel Vassel puts it well:

> The history of Christian evangelism before the colonial era was characterized by cultural sensitivity and the adaptation of the message to the receiver culture. This is demonstrated, for instance, in Christianity's classical and persistent formulation of Christology in the form of Greek ideas which is epitomized in the 'standard' creeds such as the Chalcedonian formula. This formula is loaded with Greek categories of thought, because of the Greek ethos and mind set in which it was formed. . . . Christian faith adapted itself to the new environment and addressed the question of the new ethos and answered them in the form that the culture asked them.[61]

The immigrant church is able to respect the receiver culture, resist it in the new prophetic imagination that it brings, and be an agent of redemption and a model of recreation in the new culture. The Kingdom is already and not yet. Wherever and whenever we are consistent with God's plan for the whole human family, we catch and project glimpses of the *eschaton*. We are an eschatological sign as we seek to model the vision of Isaiah 11:6-9, where the wolf and the lamb dwell together. The immigrant church is a sign of the powerful emptying themselves and all partaking of God's shalom. We seek to form and reframe a new reality consistent with God's Kingdom. Dr. Vassel's insights once again clearly elucidate this historical-eschatological project:

> Progress in Europe saw Christianity doing the same thing embracing and reloading pagan festivals . . . and in the process giving to the faith such important days as Christmas and Easter reloading them with their distinctive and definitive meanings. They were adopted from and adapted to cultures that celebrated these times in the year as central to their existence. Interpreting and responding to the culture's existential questions were roles that Christianity then sought sensitively to assume and this was done in terms of the Christian gospel.[62]

Strangers No More

Victor Hugo, the famous French novelist, once wrote, "There is nothing so powerful as an idea whose time has come," this volume, *E Pluribus Unum: Challenges and Opportunities in Multicultural Ministry*, is a manifestation of that idea for the Global church. Anthologies that are predicated on the reality of immigrant experiences still need a hearing and should be continuously developed and broadened. Just as Reformed, Wesleyan, Liberation theologies have dominated much of the ecclesial and academic landscapes, the realities of globalization invite us to further investigate how we treat and understand the stranger or "other" in our midst. The 21st century Church can ill afford to ignore the winds of demographic, culture, ethnic, and generational change. Indeed, Jesus was clear, the "wind blows wherever it pleases" (John 3:8), it is the task of the spiritually engaged church to seek to understand that blowing of the wind.

If journalist Thomas L. Friedman's work *The World Is Flat*[63] is correct, the forces of globalization need to be examined in light of the mission of the Global Church. How do we engage "strangers from different shores?" Emmanuel Levinas has accused much of

Western thought to be afflicted with an "allergy to the other." Perhaps the Global Church can provide an antidote by learning from the Emmaus paradigm of Luke 24. Initially, in our journeying together, we may not be recognizable or esteemed as stranger. Still, after we pray, open the Scriptures, and break bread together, our eyes can be opened and our hearts can burn within us. The stranger among us is the face of Jesus (Luke 24:32).

Homogeneity and heterogeneity are often viewed as antithetical to each other, two ideas competing for the minds and hearts of church planting practitioners. Because of this propensity the ethnic specific church struggles to find its rightful place as a legitimate expression of God's handiwork.

CHAPTER NINE

CULTURAL INTELLIGENCE: THE JOURNEY FROM THEORY TO CONCEPT

Given that the concept of CQ has only recently gained exposure as a viable tool in the attempt to navigate the mines of intercultural activities, it is necessary to provide the background and the journey that it has taken. This essay serves to provide an initial, empirical investigation of how experiences of those who have been involved in international cross-cultural initiatives could be integrated into a construct that includes the research that has been done in other pedagogical parallels.

The concept of CQ was first introduced to the social sciences and management disciplines by P. Christopher Earley and Soon Ang in 2003. The emergence of CQ was in response to a blind spot within the exuberance over the global recognition that our world had become "flat," and that seemingly cultural diversities and differences had been mitigated by the need for collaboration to achieve the bottom line of corporate profit. Much to the dismay of many within these companies, entrenched cultural differences were not "flattening out," and it portended that tension, conflicts, and misunderstanding would trump all well-intentioned efforts to optimize the forces of convergence in a flat world.

In 2004, the first symposium on CQ was organized at the *Academy of Management* annual meeting (Ang & Van Dynne, 2008). In 2006, the journal *Group and Organization Management* devoted an entire, special issue to CQ. In the same year, the first Global Conference on Cultural Intelligence was organized with experts in international management, cross-cultural psychology, cross-cultural management, social psychology, and applied linguistics. The CQ research that resulted from the GCCI has been presented to numerous organizations, including the Society for Industrial and Organizational Psychology (2005); American Psychological Association (2005); International Conference in Information Systems (2005); International Academy of Intercultural Relations Conference in Taiwan (2004); the 26th International Congress of Applied Psychology in Athens, Greece (2006); the Shanghai Conference on Cultural Intelligence in China (2006); the United States Defense Advanced Research Projects Agency (DARPA) in 2007; and the International Military Testing Association (IMTA) in 2007.

However, these activities had their antecedents. Much research had been done in an effort to understand the nuances of intelligence as a factor in effective performance of expatriates within culture as well as within different cultures.

Intelligence has been the subject of research among sociologists and anthropologists, who for many decades insisted that intelligence can only be researched as a function of one's culture and society. That is to say, a person is intelligent when he or she is skillful in maneuvering competently within the environment in which he or she resides. Two symposia in 1921 and 1986 were devoted exclusively to the development of a consensus on a workable definition of intelligence. In recent years, Cultural Intelligence (CQ) has chosen to adopt the framework developed by Sternberg (1986). This framework classifies contemporary views of intelligence as a characteristic of the individual, the context, and the interaction of the individual and the context. Rather than exploring a person's intelligence quotient fundamentally within her own culture, CQ refers to her capability to adapt effectively to new cultural contexts, and therefore, represents a form of situated intelligence, where intelligently adaptive behaviors are culturally bound to the values and beliefs of a selected society or culture.

The 75 Year Gap

The aforementioned symposia are significant in the background to CQ because of the conclusions reached during these deliberations. The 1921 symposium brought together fourteen prominent researchers in educational psychology on intelligence. Definitions of intelligence offered were wide ranging:

1. The ability to learn and adapt adequately in relatively new situations.
2. A sensory capacity for perceptual recognition, quickness, and range of flexibilities.
3. Knowledge or cognitive processes such as sensation, perception, association, memory, imagination, and judgment.
4. The involvement of non-cognitive attributes such as perseverance.

In 1986, Sternberg and Detterman brought together twenty contemporary researchers. In a radical departure from the first symposium, Sternberg developed a broad conceptual framework on intelligence to embrace and capture the various viewpoints held. To Sternberg, intelligence must be theorized and measured as an intra-individual attribute, operating within a particular context or environment other than one's own culture.

It was argued that, at the mental level, intelligence resides in the cognitive or motivational realm. At the cognition level, intelligence is defined through meta-cognitive processes. Motivational theorists focused on the argument that it is not sufficient to concentrate on the cognitive ability of the individual, but attention must be given to the underlying motivation. Meanwhile, the behavioral theorists focused on domains or contexts, in which intelligent behaviors are observed.

Moving beyond the individual focus, some researchers conceptualized intelligence at the contextual level of the environment. Intelligence is therefore seen, not as residing within the individual, but as a function of one's culture and society. Individuals, some say, do not operate or exist in a vacuum; therefore, people may be differently intelligent in different contexts, depending on the demands of these various environments. Sternberg and Berg (1986) concluded that in spite of the various strands of definitions discussed, there were six attributes of intelligence that could be agreed upon:

1. At a biological level, an intelligent person must have control and regulation over elementary sensory organs, including perception, sensation, and attention.
2. At the mental-functioning level, intelligence represents higher-level components of cognitive functioning, such as abstract reasoning, problem-solving, and decision-making.
3. Intelligence must embrace meta-cognitive and executive processes. One must exercise the ability to know how to know.

4. An intelligent person must possess some form of crystallized, formal, learned declarative, and experiential knowledge in a particular context.
5. Intelligence must be defined in some form of overt forms of behavior, either verbal or non-verbal.
6. The content of behavior is culturally bound and is an attribute of an individual operating within the culture of an environment that defines what intelligent behavior is.

Motivation and its Importance

Most of the work on intelligence has heretofore centered on the cognitive aspects. Some, however, would argue that without motivation the other aspects of intelligence could not be activated. Only three of the 24 researchers from the 1986 convocation advanced the importance of motivation (Baron, Snow, and Zigler). These researchers posited that there is a close relation between interests and intelligence. Interests determine motivation, which in turn determines the amount of time expended in the pursuit of the acquisition of knowledge to bridge the gap with a new culture.

CQ and the Experiential Learning Theory (ELT)

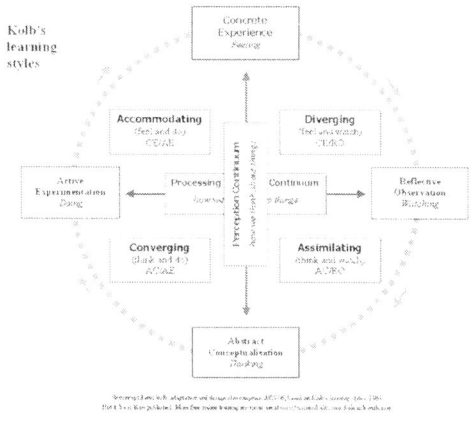

The role and significance of Experience Learning Theory (ELT) cannot be overlooked in the development of CQ, as it is advanced as a critical tool in cross-cultural ministry. In studies about the experiences of workers in global assignments, much emphasis has been placed on a performance perspective that cites the reality that these persons adjusted to their assignments and environments (Bhaskar-Shrinivas, Harrison, Shaffer, & Luk, 2005). Little, however, had been done to address the development objectives. More succinctly, no conceptual models demonstrated how these persons learned to adjust, and what types of individuals were best suited to maximize the learning curve. As a result, it became necessary to shift the focus from a performance success observation to a critical inquiry into the skills that were necessary for individuals to learn how to become effective in a different cultural environment. The model that offered a path to this investigation was that of David Kolb's (1984) experiential learning theory-- work influenced by prominent organizational scholars like John Dewey (1938), Kurt Lewin, and Jean Piaget.

The ELT structure seemed best suited to this learning process for three reasons (Ng, Van Dyne, & Ang, 2009). First, unlike the accent on the behavioral and cognitive outcomes of learning, ELT sought to unearth the intervening mechanism that transformed assignment experiences into learning outcomes. Second, ELT approached learning in a holistic fashion that integrated thinking, feeling, perceiving, and behaving as important components in the learning experience. And third, ELT places emphasis on a continuous learning dynamic that seeks to mitigate the uncertainties and complexities of new cultural environments.

From this trilogy, Kolb concluded that learning is comprised of a four-stage learning cycle further subdivided into two fundamental processes: one is *grasping* the experience, and the other is *transforming* the experience. In essence, Kolb's four-stage, ELT model prescribes a process of experiencing, reflecting, thinking, and acting. According to this line of reasoning (Kolb & Kolb), grasping without an intentional follow through (transforming) is inadequate. Therefore, events (concrete experience) form the basis for descriptive processing (reflective observation), which are followed by conceptual interpretations (abstract conceptualization), concluding with action (active experimentation).

This format is consistent with other reputable theses (Kayes et al., 2005). Consequently, unlike previously fragmented research on intercultural intelligence, Earley and Ang (2003) proposed a theoretical and economical framework that comprises four capabilities:

1. *Metacognitive CQ* is the capability to use consciousness and awareness during intercultural interactions. Those who possess high metacognitive CQ demonstrate an

ability to plan, monitor, revise, and adjust encroaching mental models (Nelson, 1996).

2. *Cognitive CQ* focuses on norms, practices, and conventions within varying cultures, including knowledge of economic, legal, and social systems of different cultures. As a consequence, persons with high cognitive CQ are more likely to make accurate interpretations of cultural interactions (Triandis, 1995).

3. *Motivational CQ* is the capability to direct attention and energy toward learning the nuances of different cultures. Such persons appreciate the importance of intrinsic value and self-efficacy, being confident of their ability to function effectively in varying cultures.

4. *Behavioral CQ* exhibits appropriate verbal and non-verbal actions based on the studied cultural values of a specific setting (Hall, 1959). Persons with high behavioral CQ display situationally appropriate behavior through appropriate words, tones, gestures, and facial expressions (Gudykunst, Ting-Tooney, & Chua, 1988).

The Nexus Between CQ and ELT

In an extensive work alluded to earlier (Ng, Dyne, and Ang), a new model of cooperation emerged that linked ELT with CQ, highlighting a correlative link between the aptitudes exhibited by successful international expatriates and their leadership styles. This link is important to the continued research in CQ, because it proposes that through the four phases of CQ, individuals could enhance the likelihood of success by the engagement of the four stages of experiential learning: concrete experience, reflective observation, abstract conceptualization, and active experimentation.

Concrete Experience (CE) – Individuals can be decisively affected by intercultural interactions, depending on the level of interest and motivation that such experiences evoke. If there is much interest generated in the midst of these interactions (Yamazaki and Kayes, 2004), the degree of involvement is enriched, and the quality of the relationship will yield predictable outcomes. These experiences in the midst of another culture require people to display flexibility and adaptability, since the norms of appropriate behavior must be continuously assessed and interpreted. From this observation, it could be proposed that *Motivational CQ and Behavioral CQ enhance the likelihood that individuals will seek and enjoy concrete cross-cultural experiences.*

Reflective Observation (RO) – Information processing is an invaluable asset for those working cross-culturally. A plethora of mistakes is made by those who do not possess the tools to interpret the social behaviors and assumptions of another's culture, and therefore lack the awareness and significance of cues that might be important to that culture. Persons with high metacognitive CQ can navigate these waters with apt consideration of the multiple perspectives that could be applicable. From this observation, it could be proposed that *Cognitive CQ and Metacognitive CQ enhance the likelihood that individuals will reflect on their cross-cultural experiences.*

Abstract Conceptualization (AC) – Research in cognitive psychology has informed us that when the knowledge gathered about another culture is properly organized and interpreted, the insights and reflections made have a greater possibility of being correct (Chase & Simon, 1973; Chi, Glaser, & Rees, 1982). The emphasis in this modality is much more scientific (thinking) as opposed to an intuitive (feeling) approach (Kolb, 1984). From this observation, it could be proposed that *Cognitive CQ and Motivational CQ enhance the likelihood that individuals will detect patterns and develop conceptual generalizations of cross-cultural experiences.*

Active Experimentation (AE) – All four facets of CQ contribute to the influencing of the environment and affect the cross-cultural experimentation. Cognitive and Metacognitive CQ enhancement enables individuals to examine ideas and suppositions; Motivational CQ, given that self-efficacy is gained through knowledge of the culture, enables the individual to persist in the midst of cultural discomfort. Through appropriate Behavioral CQ, a person can implement both verbal and non-verbal actions, even when there is minimal language skill. From this observation, it could be proposed that *all components of CQ enhance the likelihood that individuals will implement and test their conceptual generalizations in cross-cultural situations.*

Enhancement of CQ through ELT in Cross-cultural Practice

Considering the fast-paced nature of missions, its future will increasingly depend on the on the job training (OJT) that experiences bring to bear on the success or failure of the mission. As has been documented, CQ is a multidimensional approach that is best enhanced through the four dimensions of ELT. However, Kolb's contribution (1984) to the science of learning would be incomplete without his extended application of these experiential factors to what has become known as Kolb's *learning styles or abilities – feeling, thinking, reflecting, and acting.*

Experiential learning is a holistic process that combines learning abilities with the four dimensions of CE, RO, AC, and AE. Concrete Experience (feeling) abilities require the individual to deal with immediate human situations in a subjective manner, and emphasize the ability to employ feeling, intuitive understanding in the present reality, and sensitivity toward other people's emotions and values. Individuals strong in CE abilities excel at relating to people with an open mind, value interpersonal relations, and perform well in unstructured and ambiguous situations.

Conversely, AC (thinking) abilities—the dialectic opposite of CE—engage the use of logic, ideas, and concepts. Abstract Conceptualization abilities require thinking, analyzing, and building general theories. Individuals with strong AC abilities are good at making systematic plans, manipulating abstract symbols, and using quantitative analysis. Meticulousness, the rigidity of analyzing ideas, the scientific approach, and the quality of a neat theoretical model are valuable to individuals with an AC point of reference.

Reflective Observation (reflecting) abilities require understanding the meaning of thoughts and situations by cautiously watching and listening. Reflective Observation emphasizes the use of reflective understanding to discover the rationale behind the way things are. Persons strong in RO excel at imagining the meaning of situations and ideas, seeing things from different perspectives, and appreciating different opinions. They value persistence, fairness, and considered, thoughtful conclusion.

In contrast, the AE (acting) abilities emphasize actively influencing people and affecting situations. Active Experimentation focuses on practical applications and matter-of-fact focus on what works. Those with AE abilities are willing to take risks, to get things done, and to take responsibility for accomplishing objectives. Individuals with strong AE style are good at taking actions to influence their external environment and like to see results.

Associated Learning Styles and Definitions

To understand why different persons react differently in varying cultural contexts, it may be important to delve into Kolb's analysis of preferred learning styles. A combination of two learning abilities constitutes an associated learning style (Kolb, 1984; Kolb & Fry, 1975). *Learning style* denotes an individual's predilection for using two sets of learning abilities over another. The *diverging learning style* prefers CE and RO, while the *converging learning style* prefers AC and AE; the *assimilating learning style* prefers AC and RO; whereas, the *accommodating learning style* prefers CE and AE.

It is important to note that a learning style results from the interplay between the person and the environment. Thus, while learning style arises primarily from individual characteristics, style is also shaped by social, cultural, and environmental forces.

Knowing a person's (and your own) learning style enables learning to be orientated according to the preferred method. That said, everyone responds to and needs the stimulus of all types of learning styles to one extent or another - it's a matter of using emphasis that fits best with the given situation and a person's learning style preferences.

Here are brief descriptions of the four Kolb's associated learning styles:

Diverging (feeling and watching - CE/RO) – This group is able to view situations from different perspectives. They are sensitive. They would rather watch than do, tending to gather information and use imagination to solve problems. They are best at viewing concrete situations from several different viewpoints. Kolb called this style "Diverging," because these people perform better in situations that require idea-generation, for example, brainstorming. People with a Diverging learning style have broad cultural interests and like to gather information. They are interested in people, tend to be imaginative and emotional, and tend to be strong in the arts. People with the Diverging style prefer to work in groups, to listen with an open mind, and to receive personal feedback.

Assimilating (watching and thinking - AC/RO) – This group's learning preference is for a concise, logical approach. Ideas and concepts are more important than people. They require good, clear explanation rather than practical opportunity. They excel at understanding wide-ranging information and organizing it into a clear, logical format. People with an Assimilating learning style are less focused on people and more interested in ideas and abstract concepts. People with this style are more attracted to logically sound theories than approaches based on practical value. In formal learning situations, people with this style prefer readings, lectures, exploring analytical models, and having time to think things through.

Converging (doing and thinking - AC/AE) - Persons with a Converging learning style can solve problems and will use their learning to find solutions to practical issues. They prefer technical tasks and are less concerned with people and interpersonal aspects. People with a Converging learning style are best at finding practical uses for ideas and theories. They can solve problems and make decisions by finding solutions to questions and problems. People with a Converging learning style are more attracted to technical tasks and problems than social or interpersonal issues. People with a Converging style like to experiment with new ideas, to simulate, and to work with practical applications.

Accommodating (doing and feeling - CE/AE) - The Accommodating learning style is "hands-on" and relies on intuition rather than logic. This group would use other people's analysis and prefer to take a practical, experiential approach. They are attracted to new challenges and experiences and to carrying out plans. They commonly act on intuition rather than logical analysis. Persons with an Accommodating learning style will tend to rely on others for information, rather than carry out their own analysis. This learning style is prevalent and useful in roles requiring action and initiative. People with an Accommodating learning style prefer to work in teams to complete tasks. They set targets and actively work in the field, trying different ways to achieve an objective.

As with any behavioral model, this is a guide, and not a strict set of rules. Nevertheless, most people clearly exhibit strong preferences for a given learning style. The ability to use or "switch between" different styles is not one that we should assume comes easily or naturally to many people. This is important to note, because it contributes to the manner in which people respond to different stimuli cross-culturally.

Basically, people who have a clear learning style preference, for whatever reason, will tend to learn more effectively, if learning is orientated according to their preference. For instance, people who prefer the Assimilating learning style will not be comfortable being thrown in at the deep end without notes and instructions. People who prefer to use an Accommodating learning style are likely to become frustrated, if they are forced to read lots of instructions and rules and are unable to get hands-on experience as soon as possible.

Conclusion

Cultural Intelligence is more than merely a lens through which one can view the challenges posed by attempting to be successful in commerce, business, missions, and interpersonal cultural interactions. It is a research-based, interdisciplinary meta-model that provides the necessary handles for understanding why some persons adapt easily when placed in different cultures, and why others do not. The academic journey into the significance of Kolb's approach to Experiential Learning Theory should anchor us to the notion that CQ is an evolving exercise in learning from the experiences in particular situations. The four dimensions of CQ are not designed to be a linear exercise. However, each plays a pivotal role in enhancing one's competency in the interaction within cultures. Agility and flexibility will only serve the situation well after deep reflection upon the cues generated from the experience, and the sooner one can analyze what's going on, and why, the more successful he or she will be in advancing mission accomplishment.

References

Bhaskar-Shrinivas, P., Harrison, D. A., Shaffer, M. A., & Luk, D. M. 2005. Input-based and Time-based Models of International Adjustment: Meta-analytic Evidence and Theoretical Extensions. *Academy of Management Journal*, 482: 25-281.

Chase, W. G., & Simon, H. A. 1973. The Mind's Eye in Chess. In W. G. Chase (Ed.), *Visual Information Processing*: 215-281. New York: Academic Press.

Chi, M. T. H., Glaser, R., & Rees, E. 1982. *Advances in the Psychology of Human Intelligence*, 1:7-75. Hillsdale, NJ: Laurence Erlbaum Associates.

Dewey, J. 1938. *Experience and Education*. New York: Simon & Schuster.

Earley, P. C., & Ang, S. 2003. *Cultural Intelligence: Individual Interactions across Cultures*. Palo Alto, CA: Stanford University Press.

Gudykunst, W. B., Ting-Toomey, S., & Chua, E. 1988. *Culture and Interpersonal Communications*. Newbury Park, CA: Sage.

Hall, E. T. 1959. *The Silent Language*. New York: Doubleday.

Kayes, D. C., Kayes, A. B., & Yamazaki, Y. 2005. Essential Competencies for Cross-cultural Knowledge Absorption. *Journal of Management Psychology*, 20: 678-589.

Kolb, D. A. 1984. *Experiential Learning: Experience as the Source of Learning and Development*. Englewood Cliffs, NJ: Prentice Hall.

Kolb, A. Y., & Kolb, D. A. 2005. Learning Styles and Learning Spaces: Enhancing Experiential Learning in Higher Education. *Academy of Management Learning and Education*, 4: 193-212.

Kolb, D. A., & Fry, R. (1975). Toward an applied theory of experiential learning. In C. Cooper, (Ed.), *Theories of group processes*. New York: Wiley.

Nelson, T. O. 1996. Consciousness and Metacognition. *American Psychologist*, 51: 112-116.

Ng, K., Van Dyne, L., & Ang, S. *Academy of Management Learning & Education*, 2009. Vol. 8, No. 4, 511-526.

Sternberg, R. J., and Berg, C. A. 1986. Quantitative Integration: Definitions of Intelligence: A Comparison of 1921 and 1986 Symposia. In R. J. Sternberg and D. K. Detterman, eds., *What is Intelligence? Contemporary Viewpoints on its Nature and Definition*, 155-62. Norwood, N.J.: Ablex.

Sternberg, R. J., & Detterman, D. K. (Eds.). *What is Intelligence?: Contemporary Viewpoints on its Nature and Definition*. Norwood, NJ: Ablex.

Triandis, H. C. 1995. Culture Specific Assimilators. In S. M. Fowler (Ed), *Intercultural Sourcebook: Cross-cultural Training Methods*: 179-186. Yarmouth, ME: Intercultural Press.

CHAPTER TEN

CQ 101 – BRIDGING THE CULTURAL DIVIDE

N.B. This article is a booklet written by Oliver Phillips, and is a core component of the CQ Enhancement Seminar that is available to groups and organizations. As such, some of the material may have been duplicated in other places throughout this book.

The story is told of Robert Greenleaf, author of the widely used book, *Servant Leadership*, who had made a casual visit to a mental institution. Upon writing of the visit later, Greenleaf narrated about his sense of unease by the ratio of inmates to staff in a securely locked room. There were more than fifty inmates to two orderlies. He mused to himself, "These patients were sullen and hostile looking. They were standing or sitting as isolated beings with no apparent interaction among them." To bring some measure of peace to his anxiety, or for his own security, he asked the staff psychiatrist about the safety of the orderlies. The psychiatrist offered this explanation, "Not a chance; those orderlies are quite safe. You see, it is part of the illness of those poor patients that they cannot get together on anything."[64]

It is hoped that the treatment of this delicate, yet germane topic of culture's challenges would bring us closer to bridging the gap that exists between cultures with which we are summoned to interact daily, or, at least occasionally. While the challenges are manifold, there are three objectives of this booklet:

1. To define the magnitude and scope of the differences between cultures.
2. To design and develop a strategy for equipping persons to become culturally competent.
3. To commence the journey of bridging the gap with the confidence that growth in cultural awareness is a present possibility.

We welcome you as a sojourner on this pilgrimage to make our world a friendlier and more conciliatory habitat in which to live! Let's get together!

Ministry today, whether globally or locally, is fraught with the challenges presented by cultural differences. If the world were a village of 1,000 people:

- 206 would be Chinese
- 167 would be Indian
- 79 would be from Central and South America
- 50 would be from the former Soviet Union (Eastern Europe)
- 51 would be North American
- 45 would be Western European
- 33 would be Indonesian
- 21 would be from Japan
- 22 would be from Bangladesh
- 21 would be from Nigeria
- 24 would be from Pakistan
- 118 would be from other Asian countries.[65]

Religiously, the global village would look like this:

- Christian: 330, leaving 670 non-Christians
- Muslim: 198
- Nonreligious: 126
- Hindu: 135
- Buddhist: 60
- Ethno religionist: 38
- Atheist: 25
- New-religionist: 17
- Sikh: 4
- Jewish: 2
- Other: 65[66]

SECTION 1

DEFINING THE CULTURAL DIVIDE

Recently, I was in transit from London, Ontario, having just completed a CQ Enhancement Seminar at a congregation that hosted 28 different nations. While awaiting the arrival of a shuttle that would take me from the International Concourse to Concourse 2, where I would board a plane to Kansas City, I overheard a dialogue between an impatient attendant and a group of Asian tourists, who were seeking directions, due to apparently confusing signage. The attendant, frustrated by the difficulty, finally blurted out, rather tongue in cheek, "I am not always right, but I'm never wrong!" Such comedic arrogance, sadly enough, is often characteristic of attempts to bridge the cultural divide: the subject of this booklet.

The divide among cultures is not superficial; it's real! The time has come, according to recent U.S. Census statistics, when interaction with peoples from other cultures has become an everyday occurrence, rather than an occasional encounter. Without humility, a good dose of it, it is possible that, rather than closing the gap between the cultures through intentional understanding, one could easily further alienate others, or worse yet, permanently erode the foundational premises that are necessary to achieving the harmony that future partnerships require. Olive oil and water, to cite a metaphor used by Brooks Peterson, do not make naturally for a good mixture; however, when inserted appropriately in a favorite dish, can work wonders to the palate.

Culture, if it is to be cogently appreciated, must be clearly defined. Yet, the truth is that to define culture is also to recognize the existence of a great divide, a tragic gap or chasm that must be bridged. A common mistake made by most attempts is to relegate culture to a geographic location, like West coast, Southern states, Central America, and even to go so far as to talk of Asian, African, or Eastern culture. This is a good start, but culture is much more. Culture is a totality of contributory elements: behavior patterns, values, assumptions, foods, beliefs, music, institutions, and most assuredly, the product of human ingenuity and necessary for survival. This signifies that our environment is shaped and patterned by the whole of human activity. Anthropologist Clifford Geertz notes that our knowledge of culture grows in spurts. He says, "Culture is not inherited like a genetic code. Instead, culture becomes layers and layers added by our society and our surrounding environment."[67] Culture, therefore, is foundational in life. It indicates that we are a tapestry of a transmitted pattern of meanings, embodied in symbols, a system of inherited conceptions expressed in symbolic forms, by which [we] communicate, perpetuate, and develop our knowledge about and attitudes toward life.[68]

The word culture comes from the Latin *colere,* which means to cultivate. What do we cultivate? We cultivate a product that operates on three levels: (1) behaviors that are learned, (2) ideas that reinforce beliefs and values, and (3) products that reinforce beliefs. Viewed from these three levels, it is safe to suggest that these products reinforce a cultural belief system and arise out of and reflect a set of underlying ideas and values.

In common conversation, the most frequently traveled path to defining culture is the use of metaphors: "culture is like..." Such an approach reveals a plethora of analogies that present a wide array of definitions, leaving one overwhelmed by the scope of culture's tentacles.

For the present, we will use Brooks Peterson's operational definition: "Culture is the relatively stable set of <u>inner values</u> and beliefs generally held by groups of people in countries or regions and the <u>noticeable impact</u> those values and beliefs have on the peoples' <u>outward behavior and environment</u>."[69] Let's take it apart. The inner values are accrued over time, and they constitute the non-negotiable elements of a culture. They are rarely perceptible, but they have been forged by a culture through adaptation and experience. However, they are released like atomic energy in the behaviors that one notices in the culture we encounter. The recognition of the impact of these values can be the answer to building a bridge to the unfamiliar culture.

What are some of those images that describe culture? What are the images that validate and expose the complexity of the cultural gap? They are the quilt, the tree, the iceberg, and the computer.

Culture is like a handmade quilt. A well-crafted quilt is the result of the imaginative genius of human creativity. Each choice of fabric contributes uniquely to the whole; without which, the quilt is incomplete. In every culture, one finds a variety of factors, contributions to the whole that cannot be ignored. There's language, food, spirituality, laws, history, superstitions, customs, economics, politics, religion, education, health, love and marriage, family traditions, community, travel, just to mention a few. The complexity of this finished product we call culture cannot be underestimated.

Culture is like a tree. One thing we know for certain about a tree is that there are parts we can see, and parts that are hidden from the casual observer. Furthermore, trees change from year to year, depending on their environment. They adapt to the supply of rain, sunlight, wind, nutrients, but they remain essentially a tree. No one ignores the importance of the roots of the tree, the necessary pruning of the branches, and like human beings, they have basic needs like shelter, food, clothing, and relationships. Yet, every tree is so different from the tree a few yards away. A gap exists, and the tree would be the first to admit that the oak is not a maple, and the pine tree is not a pecan tree.

Culture is like an iceberg. Even in tropical countries, most persons have a sense of the subtleties of the iceberg. One inescapable global characteristic of the iceberg is that there is a part you see, and a part you don't. The cultural divide is accentuated, because no discussion of a culture can reasonably take place without recognition of the "under the water" phenomenon. The tragedy of most encounters with another culture is to deal only with the part of the iceberg that can be seen, ignoring the 80% that is submerged. Any discussion with persons who anticipate a trip to a new culture, or who interact with individuals in the workplace is couched with the questions, "What do they look like?" "Are they friendly?" "How's the food?" But that is only the tip of the iceberg!

The tip of the iceberg might make for interesting and exciting conversation, but the "below the surface" realities present intractable values that determine behavior and the environment.

Culture is like the computer. Technologically, culture could also be viewed as the collective programming of the mind that distinguishes the members of one group or category of people from others. To put it simply, culture is the software of the mind.[70] On your computer, hardware does not determine the computer's programming; this is accomplished by the downloaded software . The software gives a specific function and a specific type of production to the computer. As such, culture will determine patterns of thinking, feeling, and acting. When culture is viewed as a computer, we begin to get a glimpse of the divide that exists, because of the different software packages that are to be found in every culture.

The bridging of the divide is the primary focus of this booklet, because too many persons and groups of people ignore the existence of the divide. This divide creates linguistic, spatial, intracultural, and intercultural challenges, and the proceeding sections will attempt to provide an adequate toolkit to build that bridge.

However one conceives of the complexity of culture, we are all summoned to reshape human and social interactions to manage the stress of culture shock and the subsequent frustrations that typically result from facilitating effective cross-cultural adjustments. Before the bridge can be effectively built, several questions could be raised:

1. How do individuals develop their ability to adapt effectively across different cultures?
2. Why do some individuals possess superior capacity to deal with the challenges of working in cultures?
3. How do individuals reach full productive potential working in culturally diverse work environments in their home countries and abroad?
4. How do organizations build the capacity for effective global work assignments in different locations around the world?
5. How do organizations optimize individual and collective performance by harnessing the cultural diversity of their people across the world?

EQ, according to Mayer and Salovey, refers to a complex set of characteristics: "the ability to perceive emotions, to access and generate emotions so as to assist thought, to understand emotions and emotional knowledge, and to reflectively regulate emotions so as to promote emotional and intellectual growth" (1997, 5).

CQ is best defined as the capability to function effectively across various cultural contexts (national, ethnic, organizational, generational, etc.)[71] Cultural Intelligence is not a quick fix. Neither is this booklet designed to make you an expert in CQ, once the contents have been digested. For as long as you continue to interact with persons and institutions with cultures of their own making, you will continue to make small or large mistakes. CQ is not about simply adapting and changing our patterns and personality, nor is it about acquiring specific skill sets. Life is too complicated for such simple elixirs. CQ is fundamentally about changing our view of culture in a manner that honors differences in cultures other than our own. It is about creating **systemic change** that respects where others are, without trying to move them to where we would like them to be.

Nobody ever really behaves flawlessly in cross-cultural situations. We are always learning. However, persons with low CQ stand out conspicuously, maybe because we become used to laughing at occasional faux pas. The corporate world is filled with cultural advertising gaffes that resulted in very embarrassing moments for those involved. A few years ago, the American Dairy Association led a wildly successful marketing campaign throughout the U.S. built upon the slogan, "Got Milk?" Unfortunately, when the campaign was exported to Mexico, the translation read, "Are you lactating?"[72] A U.S. software company suffered from having the name of their industry translated as an "underwear" company when launching internationally. A European company couldn't succeed selling their chocolate and fruit dessert called "Zit" in the United States, nor could the Fins who attempted to sell "Super Piss," a Finnish product for unfreezing car door locks. There are countless other examples like these.

We are told that low CQ is the overwhelming reason why international initiatives fail, resulting in an estimated loss of millions of dollars. In fact, 90% of leading executives from 68 countries name cross-cultural leadership **as** the top management challenge for the next century.[73] Businesses and organizations that cite CQ as an important factor in the day-to-day operations have a distinct competitive advantage that translates into long-term profitability. Consider these realities:

- Teachers with high CQ learn how to adapt their teaching, assessment, and feedback strategies, when working with students from various cultural backgrounds.
- Human resource managers with higher levels of CQ have a better sense of how to handle a Muslim employee's request to miss a sales conference during Ramadan.
- Hospitals led by culturally intelligent leaders are more effective at treating immigrant patients and have fewer lawsuits due to misdiagnosis of those patients.
- Students with higher CQ, who volunteer or study abroad, gain long-term benefits from the experience.
- Liberals and conservatives with high CQ temper their broad, sweeping statements about one another, seek to understand the other party's position, and learn where the true differences lie, rather than sensationalizing artificial polarities.[74]

SECTION 2

DISMANTLING CULTURAL ASSUMPTIONS

Before a bridge can be built between cultures, it is necessary to address some assumptions about culture that, if ignored, may spell disaster, or worse yet, make the construction of the bridge impossible. There are some glaring, entrenched assumptions that must be debunked.

First Assumption – all people within a particular culture are the same. The temptation is to place people in a box with inflexible labels that correlate to actions, behavior, and values. CQ provides conclusions on cultures or groups of people, but it does not stereotype. Stereotyping is usually a negative statement, when a blanket perception is applied to an entire group of people. For example, we may know one Jamaican person who is very loud; consequently, we conclude that all Jamaicans are loud and boisterous. A stereotype is an incorrect observation of a people, based on minimal experiential evidence.

Second Assumption – we could live in a color-blind society. The advocates of a color- blind society were well-intentioned, hoping that we would have a society in which individuals would not be judged solely on the color of their skin. The truth of the matter is that such an attitude perpetuates the assumption that we would ignore the historical context, in which people of different races and cultures exist, thereby giving credence to the pseudo-scientific premise of the inferiority of one particular race.

Third Assumption – America is a melting pot. While the concepts sound harmless enough, the idea of a homogeneous American culture can only exist when we ignore — or worse, forget — the history that has shaped this country. The time was when immigrants to this country were far removed from their homeland by geography and time. This is no longer the case. Because of vastly improved travel technology, inexpensive air flights, ethnic shopping and marketing, and the like, immigrants are more and tradition.

Fourth Assumption – cultural intelligence cannot be learned. Most scholars of the science of intelligence would suggest that one's IQ is fixed, and cannot be improved. One's IQ at age seven is assumed to be the same at age twenty-seven. Be that as it may, one's CQ can be improved through intervention, since cultural intelligence is believed to be malleable. Through interventions like those discussed in this booklet, we can develop our aptitude for interacting with the persons of other cultures in ways that are loving and respectful. Surely some people are more naturally gifted for cross-cultural work, just as some individuals are more naturally inclined toward engineering, art, or fixing things around the house. But almost everyone can make progress in becoming more effective cross-culturally.

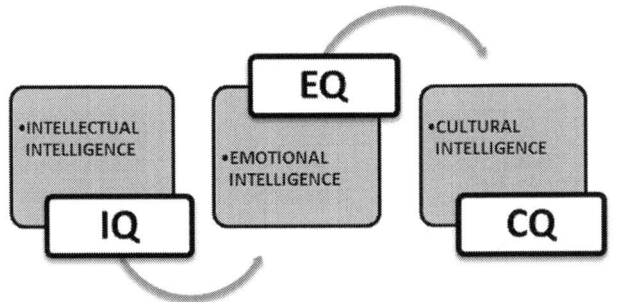

Fifth Assumption – people from other cultures act randomly or stupidly. Understanding is the ability to see patterns and values that reveal the integrity of a people. Lack of understanding leads to false assumptions.

Duane Elmer tells of an incident in Kenya with the Maasai people: the Maasai elder was in the midst of Elmer's group during a visit, and he told his son to do whatever the Maasai elder asked of him. As the Maasai elder approached, the youngest son, Marc, did as he had been told: "Step forward and bow your head. The elder will put his hand on your head and offer a greeting." It was the way for Maasai children, and they would honor their ways. The Maasai elder proceeded to spit on his head three times. Confusion flooded their minds, as they tried to understand what had just happened. Then, Marc stepped back to his mother's side and said, "Mom that man spit on me. He spit on me." His mother answered, "Yes, we must wait and see what it means," and the elder stepped forward to greet them in a more traditional Western way. Later, they asked a friend who knew the Maasai how they should interpret the spitting on their son. He laughed and said, "It was a blessing. They do it all the time." Their son didn't feel blessed, and they were skeptical. But with further information, they began to understand. The Maasai believe that when it rains on their heads and land, God is spitting - God is blessing them.[75] I have learned that the Maasai people also spit in their hands before a handshake to seal a business deal, and they also spit on babies, when they are first brought into the public.

Sixth Assumption – we have a mandate to transform other people's culture and eliminate unethical practices. "Guanxi" (pronounced (*gwan-shee*) is one of the most powerful forces in Chinese culture. Guanxi expresses an obligation of one party to another or one person to another. More significantly, it expresses an obligation of one person to another over time. To have quanxi with another is to be available to reciprocate through a favor sometime in the future, depending on the depth of the relationship.

In that culture, quanxi with another person is like a debt owed that will be paid sometime in the future. To outsiders, this is often interpreted as a bribe. Oh, this is such gross misunderstanding! The exchange of favors does not have to be in like kind. So, if one person helps introduce you to someone, it is not beyond the scope of the relationship for that party to then ask you to help get a visa to your country, or get their son into a foreign school.

Failure to repay favors in this type of relationship is equivalent to not paying a financial obligation. If one cannot accommodate a specific request, one must find another way to make amends, perhaps by sending along a small gift to let the party know you are sorry you could not help, and that you still want to maintain the relationship.

Blundering Through Wrong Assumptions

When our assumptions are ill-founded, blunders are very often the result. Here are a few blunders that could have been avoided with a heightened understanding of the culture:

- An American oil rig supervisor in Indonesia shouted at an employee to take a boat to shore. Since no one berates an Indonesian in public, a mob of outraged workers chased the supervisor with axes.

- Pepsodent tried to sell its toothpaste in Southeast Asia by emphasizing that it "whitens your teeth." They found out that the local natives chew betel nuts to blacken their teeth, which they find attractive.

- A company advertised eyeglasses in Thailand by featuring a variety of cute animals wearing glasses. The ad was a poor choice, since animals are considered to be a form of low life and no self-respecting Thai would wear anything worn by animals.

- The soft drink Fresca was promoted by a saleswoman in Mexico. She was surprised that her sales pitch was greeted with laughter, and later embarrassed when she learned that fresca is slang for "lesbian."

- A soft drink was introduced into Arab countries with an attractive label that had stars on it: six-pointed stars. The Arabs interpreted this as pro-Israeli and refused to buy it. Another label was printed in ten languages, one of which was Hebrew. Again, the Arabs did not buy it.

- U.S. and British negotiators found themselves at a standstill when the American company proposed that they "table" particular key points. In the U.S. "tabling a motion" means to not discuss it, while the same phrase in Great Britain means to "bring it to the table for discussion."

- Kellogg had to rename its Bran Buds cereal in Sweden, when it discovered that the name roughly translated to "burned farmer."
- When PepsiCo advertised Pepsi in Taiwan with the ad, "Come Alive with Pepsi" they had no idea that it would be translated into Chinese as "Pepsi brings your ancestors back from the dead."
- American medical containers were distributed in Great Britain and caused quite a stir. The instructions to, "Take off top and push in bottom," innocuous to Americans, had very strong sexual connotations to the British.
- In Italy, a campaign for Schweppes Tonic Water translated the name into "Schweppes Toilet Water."
- In a Belgrade hotel elevator: To move the cabin, push the button for wishing floor. If the cabin should enter more persons, each one should press a number of wishing floor. Driving is then going alphabetically by national order.
- In a Yugoslavian hotel: The flattening of underwear with pleasure is the job of the chambermaid.
- In a Bangkok dry cleaner's: Drop your trousers here for best results.
- In an East African newspaper: A new swimming pool is rapidly taking shape, since the contractors have thrown in the bulk of their workers.
- Detour sign in Kyushi, Japan: Stop--Drive sideways.
- At a Budapest zoo: Please do not feed the animals. If you have any suitable food, give it to the guard on duty.

Poor cross-cultural awareness has many consequences, some serious, others comical. It is imperative that in the global economy cross-cultural awareness is seen as a necessary investment to avoid such blunders as we have seen above.[76]

Incorrect assumptions result from thinking that one's knowledge of a culture is sufficient to maneuver through the deeper values and customs inherent in the culture. There's more to the iceberg than the surface. Adeptness within one's own culture is no guarantee that the cultural difference could be easily mitigated.

Assumptions are the nucleus for breakdown in communication, be they verbal or nonverbal.

American manager, John Potts, operates a maquiladora just inside Arizona's border with Mexico. His American employees have always considered him to be sympathetic and sensitive to their needs. As a way to get to know his Mexican workforce better, Potts arranged a dinner at his house and invited three of his Mexican managers. After refusing the invitation several times, the managers agreed to take him up on the offer. From his perspective, the dinner went well, and he felt that the experience opened new doors of communication.

One week after the dinner, two of the managers quit. Potts was disheartened. What signals had he missed? What might he have said that offended the managers? What protocols did he violate in inviting them to his home? What was it about the food that he and his wife served?

Later, Potts learned that it was nothing that he had said. However, the dinner lowered the power distance between him and these managers; the act of socializing with them ran counter to the cultural work environment, and the managers feared that they might be expected to do the same with their workers, and that doing so would make it difficult for them to demand the respect and loyalty from them that they felt they deserved. Removal of the power distance was alien to the men's culture, and Potts' invitation destroyed an element that was an essential tool for effective management in that culture. While he was seen as an empathetic boss in his own culture, in the Mexican managers' culture, he was seen as weak. He missed the cues that should have alerted him to these significant differences.

SECTION 3

DEVELOPING A CULTURAL INTELLIGENCE STRATEGY

Much research has been done in the area of intelligence. No one doubts the fact that intelligence can offer the competitive advantage in a world where success is measured by one's ability to achieve goals and aspirations. This search for getting a handle on the significance of intelligence first led researchers and academicians to delve into the role that IQ plays in the marketplace. They concluded that IQ, or one's cognitive capabilities, was a sound predictive measurement of the possibility of success. As time passed, it was discovered that persons with high IQ sometimes are not sufficiently balanced emotionally or socially to be successful; hence, the attention was directed towards the importance of EQ measurement, or emotional intelligence or capabilities.

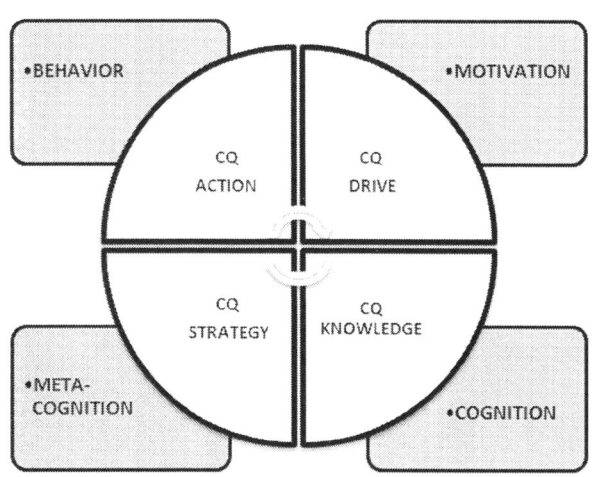

Soon researchers had to admit that while IQ and EQ could predict the possibility of success, they both were observed within the framework of a similar culture. The question then became, "Why do some people interact successfully within their own culture, and fail miserably outside of those boundaries?" Thus was born CQ or Cultural Intelligence.

A person with high CQ could be effective in bridging the gap between cultures – whether on a mission trip, in intimate relationships, the workplace, school, or any situation that calls for cultural interaction. How does one become culturally competent?

Motivation – one must begin the task of bridging the gap by asking the question, *"Do I have the confidence and motivation to work through the challenges and conflict that inevitably accompany cross-cultural situations?"* A casual interest in enjoying a trip to a different country, or experiencing different palates, or flamboyant encounters with another culture would prove to be a disastrous path to building bridges.

Frustration is the common experience of those who interact with other cultures, and perseverance only comes through a heightened level of confidence that one possesses the capacity to be adaptive. In the business world, it is important to keep sight of the bottom line. In relationships, one visualizes what harmony might look like. Our CQ Drive could be greatly enhanced by staying connected to the impulses that initiated exploration in the first place.

Knowledge – it is important to gather lots of information about one's own culture, as well as of the other. A common mistake is to plunge headlong into becoming knowledgeable about the new culture, while one is not clear about what describes one's own culture. Once one understands her culture, the question to be asked is, *"Do I have the cultural understanding necessary to be more effective cross-culturally?"* This by no means should imply that one has to master all the ins and outs of every culture. But it does mean that one must have a holistic, well-organized understanding of what makes that culture what it is, and what are the values and assumptions that inform behavior.

What knowledge does one need? And how does one become knowledgeable? To begin with, nothing can be a substitute for hands-on experience within the culture. Authentic knowledge cannot be gained from a distance! In the acquisition of this knowledge, be aware of the universal values that each culture chooses to adhere to. Here are a few:

1. *Individualism -- Collectivism* – highly individualist cultures, such as the United States or Australia, emphasize the rights and responsibilities of the individual. Collectivist cultures like China and Jordan prioritize the rights and needs of groups.[77]
2. *Power Distance* – low power-distance cultures such as Israel and Canada diminish the significance of formal titles and roles and prefer flat organizational charts. High power-distance cultures such as India and Brazil think titles and clear authority lines are important indicators of how to relate and behave.[78]
3. *Uncertainty Avoidance* – low uncertainty avoidance cultures such as Hong Kong and the United Kingdom have a higher tolerance and comfort with ambiguity and risk. High uncertainty avoidance cultures such as Russia and Japan look for ways to prevent uncertainty and risk.[79]

4. *Cooperativeness – Competitiveness* – cultures that have a cooperative orientation such as Chile and the Netherlands value a more collaborative, nurturing approach to situations. Cultures with a more competitive orientation like Japan and Hungary have a more aggressive and assertive approach to life.[80]

5. *Time Orientation* – short-term cultures such as Australia and the United States emphasize instant results. Long-term cultures such as South Korea and Brazil are more interested in long-term innovation and success, even if it means delayed gratification.[81]

6. *Context* – low context-cultures such as Israel and Canada will usually post a lot of signs and directions and emphasize very direct, thorough communication. High-context cultures such as Saudi Arabia and Mexico presume individuals know how to get along more intuitively, where explicit communication is unnecessary.[82]

7. *Doing – Being* – doing cultures such as the United States and Austria are extremely task-focused and outcome-oriented. In contrast, being cultures such as Sweden and Brazil prioritize relationships and social networks and live for the moment.[83]

Together with the understanding of these values, one must become aware of the quirks and eccentricities in one's own culture.

Strategy -- armed now with an adequate supply of information, and being properly motivated, the question to be asked is, *"Am I aware, and can I plan appropriately in light of the personal and cultural dynamics involved?"*

There are three sub-dimensions to an effective strategy: awareness, planning, and checking.

Awareness

The story is often told of an airline that was having problems with their operations in Hong Kong. Unaware of the customs of the people, the airline decided to distribute white carnations to its passengers as a way of showing appreciation. What the airline did not realize was that to many Asians, white carnations represented death, bad luck, and suffering. Another incident worthy of reference is Chevrolet's introduction in Mexico of the Nova car. When translated, "no va" in Spanish means "no go." Such cultural blunders could have been avoided, if attention and time had been expended in studying the Mexican culture.

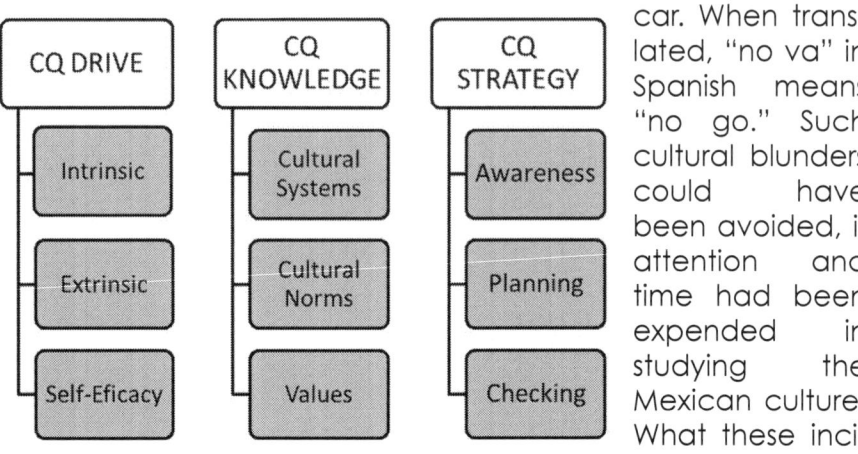

What these incidents reflect is that knowledge about a culture is much more than the acquisition of facts about a culture; these data must be interpreted at a deeper level.

Anthropologist Edward Hall relates an incident that took place on one of his early visits to Japan. Upon returning to his hotel after a visit to the mall, he noticed that all his things had been removed from his room, and he had been relocated to another room, in another section of the hotel. No mention or note was made or left in his room to explain why he had been moved. Three days later, upon returning from a corporate meeting, he had again been relocated. Not wanting to create a fuss, Hall never mentioned this bizarre action to anyone, including the manager. His assumption was that he was simply being treated as "gaijin," or a foreigner. One year later he returned to Japan, this time staying at another hotel in another part of town. In the week that he stayed on this trip, he was moved three times, this time not merely from room to room, but from hotel to hotel. This time, he complained to a friend, who told him that it was a complimentary gesture. The Japanese will never move strangers around, only friends or family.

Hadn't Hall been aware, he never would have reacted in the manner he did. Let's look at another example of strategic thinking. This illustration is that of a young Black professional woman from Brooklyn, New York, who was assigned by her utilities' company to Cairo, Egypt. As she was walking the street, she was confronted by a group of young men, who used a word that she thought was offensive.

> I turned on my heel, went right up to the group of guys, and began to upbraid them as vituperatively as my Arabic would allow. These young men were obviously shocked at my reaction, as I am sure they thought they were greeting me in a friendly way. And once I'd had my say, I stormed off to meet my friend.
>
> *After I'd walked about half a block, I decided not to leave them with a cloud of disdain hanging in the air, as I would normally have done. So I went back to talk to the group in a calmer, more diplomatic manner. They asked me why I was so angry, I gave them my reasons, they apologized profusely, and we all sat down and had tea and an interesting talk about words, and how the wrong ones can easily cause trouble. This was especially helpful to all of us, as these guys were in school, and most of them were studying English, with varying levels of success. During our conversation, I brought up a number of examples of Arabic expressions that, uttered in the wrong tone or by the wrong person, would spark an equal reaction from them. After about hour together, I had a group of new friends.*[84]

This incident illustrates two important features of the young woman's cultural awareness. First, she did not simply get angry; she returned and engaged the group in a conversation that reaped rewards. And secondly, she had noticed that their reaction to her anger was one of confusion and hesitation. Being aware, she picked up a signal that served to enhance her understanding of the culture and thus helped to build the cultural bridge. Learning about the new culture, and with openness on both sides, heightened sensitivity to different cultural contexts, as well as an awareness of a different perspective on cross-cultural engagement. Being aware paid off!

Let's look at another example. "Imagine that this is your first encounter with an Ashanti businessman from central Ghana. A friendly form of greeting in Ashanti culture is to clasp hands in a handshake and slowly pull one another's hands away from each other rubbing palms together. As you do so, you move your middle finger and thumb in a 'snapping one's fingers' gesture, and as the two hands physically separate at the fingertips, each person makes a snapping sound of the interlaced middle fingers and thumbs (overlapping one another). Our astute traveler may know about this custom, be inclined to follow it, and even attempt it. However, such an action is likely to end in failure a number of times. For some people, it is not at all easy to acquire such a behavior successfully, so a culturally intelligent action is not achieved. Does this mean that our sojourner is not culturally intelligent? By our vague usage we would say, yes. It is not sufficient to have knowledge of another group's ways of dealing with the world. One must be able (and motivated) to use this knowledge and produce a culturally appropriate response."[85]

SECTION 4 –

DEPLOYING THE CULTURAL BRIDGE

It is now assumed that we are comfortable with the assumption or the premise that a great divide exists between cultures, and that the task before us is to become competent in bridging that divide. In the sections we have covered thus far, we have dismantled the faulty assumptions about culture, as well as developed a well thought out strategy and plan for the bridge we are committed to build.

My Iguana Turned into a Dog

I travelled to a certain country (which I would rather not name) for the first time, and upon arrival, was immediately at home in the tropical climate that resembled so much the island of Trinidad, where I grew up. There is something magical about the tropics. Besides the obvious absence of the wintry nights and blistering cold days, animal and bird life is a beauty to behold: the chirping of the sparrows, the colorful plumes of a variety of birds that give one the sense that birds invented color, and the fish and sea life that is simply marvelous.

And then there is wild life! I just had a compulsion to ask my designated driver, "Do you have iguanas here?" Not that I wanted one for a pet; I wanted an iguana so that my culinary vocation could be exercised and experienced. In my home, an iguana is not only an expensive occasional treat, but it is purely delightful. Your neighbors and friends are really your friends, when an iguana is curried or stewed. To my utter disappointment, my host told me that iguanas are not seen in that part of the country and are not eaten by the local population.

However, realizing that I had an adventurous streak, my host asked whether I had ever eaten dog before. In my startled response, I offered more information than I should have. I said, "I have never, and it is because I had never had the opportunity to." There was a smirk on his face, as though to say that he was going to deliver me from such experiential isolation. That night, in the midst of friendly natives, I was somewhat startled when a white bowl of meat found its way to my side of the table. **My iguana had turned into a dog.** The rest of the story is now a permanent narrative in my repertoire of CQ moments to remember.

I was deploying the cultural bridge at a moment in time that the natives were awaiting my response to their overture of friendliness and hospitality. Building the cultural bridge is fraught with moments when the decision must be made by asking the question, *"What behaviors should I adapt for this cross-cultural situation?"* Real bridge builders ultimately come to that moment, when verbal, non-verbal, and speech acts must be adapted to suit the situation, drawing from the motivation, knowledge, and strategy that have been honed for the moment of deployment.

At the end of the day, the bridge can be built based on how we behave. Knowledge, motivation, and strategy must soon be put to the test, and our actions must demonstrate that we are willing to close the gap that exists between the cultures. The task is not necessarily to alter the behavior of those of the other culture, though there are certainly times when that course of action is advisable. The task is to be least offensive by our actions, in order to learn another culture and appreciate the differences. Or to put it delicately, what do we do when the iguana turns into a dog?

As I have come to realize after much research, more people in the world have tasted dog than they have iguana. In countries where iguanas are eaten, they are known as "chicken of the tree," but they are still considered disgusting by peoples around the world. We are a world of cultures, and bridges must be built through adaptability and flexibility, rather than by judging, prejudice, and condemnation.

As you prepare to deploy the bridge across culture, the factors to be considered would be:

Non-Verbal – the extent to which you can comfortably adapt your nonverbal behavior in the cross-cultural situation (gestures and facial expressions); verbal – the extent to which you modify your verbal behavior in cross-cultural situations (accent, tone, pronunciation, and language); and speech acts – the way you alter your communication to effectively achieve a goal in a cross-cultural situation (the way you provide critique or express gratitude). Building the bridge to mitigate the divide entails the capacity to adjust and adapt to the different cultural behaviors, while at the same time remaining true to who you are as a person of culture yourself.

I would borrow eight suggestions for building the cultural bridge as taught by David Livermore in his new book, *The Cultural Intelligence Difference*.[86] Whether one is in a strange country on a short-term missions trip, reaching a new group for congregational outreach, negotiating a new cultural situation in the workplace, or encountering a person for individual evangelism, these suggestions seem to enhance cultural competency.

1. Develop a repertoire of social skills

Become acquainted with the nonverbal cues that are observed in the mannerisms of the cultural group. It is by living close to the people that a common understanding is gained about behaviors and their significance. Anthropologists seeking knowledge about a group would spend several years among the people, in an attempt to unearth nuances of a culture. A case in point is "guanxi" in Chinese culture. Guanxi is the custom of gift-giving in gratitude for the recognition of a significant relationship among the Chinese people. To the uninitiated and uninformed business person, this appears to be a bribe in an effort to grasp an advantage in negotiation. However, to ignore this practice is to weaken the bond among the people. Another example is the way an elderly or educated person is approached in the Thai culture. "Wai" is the practice of clasping the hand in a prayer position, with the fingers extended facing upward in front of one's face, and bowing slightly forward.

A lack of awareness of these idiosyncrasies in a culture can spell disaster. Spend time with a people to pick up on the nonverbal behaviors that tell a story that's much deeper than the action observed. Ask about contemporary events and the relationship between those events and the way in which people will continue to live their lives.

2. Be an actor

We often hear of some prominent person in the news media and elsewhere, who went incognito as a homeless person for a week or so. This is acting at its best, but the information gained is priceless. Likewise, one should act out situational responses in anticipation of encounters with persons of a different culture. If you were a member of that culture, how would you act in response to bad news? Imagine yourself in their shoes for a day. Practice. Practice. Practice.

A warning should be sounded here; however, be very careful that your flexibility is not judged as mimicry. This will spell disaster. The culturally competent person knows when to flex behavior to mirror that of the other person, and when not to flex. Such decision-making discretion only comes through practice and keen observation.

3. Make taboos taboo

In some Middle Eastern countries, thumbs-up is an obscene gesture, signifying where one should sit. While this is very offensive, it is a common mistake for Westerners to indicate their appreciation for a good culinary dish with such a gesture. Learn what gestures are considered taboo in the culture. Now, it is highly improbable to know all the actions that are offensive, but the attempt to become familiar with them is highly recommended, at least to avoid that embarrassing moment.

One invaluable resource to familiarize oneself with taboos from more than 60 countries is the bestselling book, *Kiss, Bow, or Shake Hands*, a book that gives expert understanding of international protocols, practices, and cultural cues.[87] Here are a few taboos from diverse cultures:

- Never photograph or touch a symbol (e.g., Krishna statue) without permission.
- Don't hand a person anything with your left hand.
- Don't touch someone on the head.
- Don't touch your feet or put them up on the furniture.
- Avoid telling jokes or trying too hard to be funny. They very rarely translate appropriately.
- Don't assume that someone shares your views about politics, sexuality, or religion.

4. Use basic vocabulary

Some are not as linguistically challenged as I am and are very adept at learning the fundamentals of a foreign language. To those of my likeminded friends, a word of caution is in order: "Learn short words and phrases!" Once you find yourself in a new culture, with a different language, it is almost inexcusable not to at least communicate through the use of some core set of phrases or words. Some crucial words are: Please, Thank you, Sorry, Yes, No, Good, Not good, Hello, Goodbye, Come here, Go there, and of course, Toilet.

Some have suggested that if it is difficult to remember these words, at least they could be written down for quick reference.

5. Try new vocal sounds

Different cultures express approval of what is being said in conversations with a great deal of variety. We Americans are used to interrupting conversations with: "hmm," "uh-huh," "right," or in my case, "sure, sure." It might be good practice to attempt to eliminate such expressions when communicating in another culture, because they may convey the opposite intended effect. Try to handle the use of sound, i.e. "louder" or "softer," when speaking.

6. **Slow down**

In building this cultural bridge to a different culture, the rate of speech is critical. Because you are really multi-tasking while speaking (searching for cues both verbal and nonverbal), it is important to slow things down a bit, so you don't miss an important cue. This does not mean that one should speak so slowly as to be irritating and rude. But it does mean that while speaking you are also reading the nonverbal signals. As Americans, we are dominated by speed and immediacy. The point to remember is that when English is not the primary language of the other person, it is surely polite to care for the communication to be effective. Like driving a car, it is extremely difficult to maneuver the sudden turns while traveling at high and unsafe speeds.

7. **Put yourself in a place of need**

How do we approach others, when we find ourselves in the minority position, when we seem to be the only ones who speak English? The remark I often hear from those reporting from a short-term mission trip is, "No one spoke English, so I had to use an interpreter," rather than, "I could not speak Dutch, so I had to use an interpreter." This attitude gives the appearance that our language remains the predominant language, in spite of the fact that, in that context, we are the only ones who are English-speaking.

I have been guilty of frantically asking that primordial survival question to a total stranger, "Do you speak English?" A more effective approach, and one that exposes our vulnerability might be, "I am sorry. I don't speak Dutch. Do you speak English?" Here are some common language translations that you might find useful:

Arabic -- *Ana aasaf. La atakellam al'arabiyya. Hel tatalellem alingleeziyya?*

Cantonese -- *Um-ho-yee-see. Ngo-umsick-gong-gwong-dung-wa. Nay sick-um-sick gong yingmun.*

Dutch -- *Ik betreur. Ik maak je geen word Nederlands. Denkt u maar Engels spreken?*

German -- *Es tut mir leid. Ich spreche kein Deutsch. Sprechen Sie Englisch?*

French -- *Je, suis désolé. Je ne parle pas de français. Parlez-vous l'anglais?*

Haitian Creole -- *Mwin regret. Mwin pa palé creol. Es ke ou palé anglè ?*

Hindi -- *Maaf karein. Main Hindi nahin jaanta. Kya aap Angrezi jaants hain?*

Italian -- *Mi dispiace. Io non parlo italiano. Lei parla inglese?*

Japanese -- *Gomen nasai. Nihongo shaberaremasen. Ego shaberaremasuka?*

Mandarin -- *Dui bu qi. Wo bu hui shou Pu Tong Hua. Ni hui shuo Ying yu ma?*

Portuguese -- *Sinto muito, mas não falo Português. Você fala Inglês*

Spanish -- *Perdón. No habla español. ¿Habla Usted ingles?*

8. Join a multicultural team.

Nothing beats the assemblage of a group of persons who reflect different perspectives, values, and circumstances. By getting a group together the comfort level is dramatically increased, and there is absolute freedom to discuss the shades and nuances of a culture.

It is imperative that one understands that becoming culturally intelligent is the ability to synthesize motivation, knowledge, strategy, and behavior in a manner that achieves the desired result. It reminds me of a story I read, as related by Soon Ang and Christopher Earley about Greg Mortenson, who wrote the book

Three Cups of Tea. "One evening in the late 1990s while visiting a village in northern Pakistan, Mortenson was kidnapped by eight men wearing masks and whisked away into the night. He was held in captivity with no contact outside of his minimal contact with his abductors. After three days in captivity, he decided that he was very worried about his fate and that he needed to do something to improve his situation. He first asked his captors for a copy of the Koran along with someone who would translate it for him. Next, he told his captors that he was married and that his wife was expecting their first child, a son. He knew from his experiences from the local culture that a firstborn child was considered a positive omen and that having a son was a sign of particularly good fortune. Therefore, killing him would be very unlucky and create bad fortune for his executioners.

After eight days of captivity, Mortenson was released (he had been abducted as a pawn in a local political fight) unharmed. Interestingly, when he was invited back by his captors to visit the area several years later, he returned and gained some closure. In discussing his captivity and his various ploys to remain alive, he found out that his captors did not really believe the story of the birth of a son, but they commented that they did appreciate his knowledge of their local culture and customs. They believed that someone who had taken the time to understand their beliefs and practices showed a commitment to the region that had to be respected."[88]

This story clearly demonstrates the need to be balanced in the attempt to become culturally intelligent. If Mortenson had used pure knowledge about the culture without regard to the underlying meaning, he might not have survived.

SECTION 5

DESIGNATIONS OF CULTURAL TERMS

Assimilation - A process of consistent integration; whereby, members of an ethno-cultural group, typically immigrants, or other minority groups, are "*absorbed*" into an established larger community

Biculturalism - The simultaneous identification with two cultures, when an individual feels equally at home in both cultures and feels emotional attachment with both cultures. The term started appearing in the 1950s.

Biethnic - Of two ethnic groups: belonging or relating to two different ethnic groups. Usually used in reference to a person.

Bilingual Education - teaching a second language by relying heavily on the native language of the speaker. The background theory claims that a strong sense of one's own culture and language is necessary to acquire another language and culture.

Biracial - Of two races. Usually used to refer to people whose parents come from two different races, e.g., father is Chinese and mother English.

Collectivism - Individualism/Collectivism is one of the Hofstede dimensions in intercultural communication studies. *"Collectivism pertains to societies in which people from birth onwards are integrated into strong, cohesive in-groups, which throughout people's lifetime continue to protect them in exchange for unquestioning loyalty"* (Hofstede, G. 1991).

Cross Cultural - Interaction between individuals from different cultures. The term cross-cultural is generally used to describe comparative studies of cultures. Inter cultural is also used for the same meaning.

Cross Cultural Awareness - Develops from cross-cultural knowledge as the learner understands and appreciates the deeper functioning of a culture.

Cross-Cultural Communication - (also referred to as *Intercultural Communication*) A field of study that looks at how people from differing cultural backgrounds try to communicate.

Cross-Cultural Competence - The final stage of cross-cultural learning; signals the individual's ability to work effectively across cultures.

Cross-Cultural Knowledge - A surface level familiarization with cultural characteristics, values, beliefs and behaviors. It is vital to basic cross-cultural understanding, and without it cross-cultural competence cannot develop.

Cross-Cultural Sensitivity - An individual's ability to read into situations, contexts, and behaviors that are culturally rooted, and consequently, the individual is able to react to them suitably.

Cultural Diffusion - The spreading of a cultural trait (e.g., material object, idea, or behavior pattern) from one society to another.

Cultural Diversity - Differences in race, ethnicity, language, nationality, or religion. Cultural diversity refers to the variety or multiformity of human social structures, belief systems, and strategies for adapting to situations in different parts of the world.

Cultural Identity - The identity of a group or culture, or of an individual as her/his belonging to a group or culture affects her/his view of herself/himself. People who feel they belong to the same culture share a common set of norms.

Cultural Imperialism - The rapid spread or advance of one culture at the expense of others, or its imposition on other cultures, which it modifies, replaces, or destroys-usually due to economic or political reasons.

Cultural Norms - Behavior patterns that are typical of specific groups, which have distinct identities, based on culture, language, ethnicity, or race separating them from other groups.

Cultural Rights - The idea that certain rights are vested not in individuals but in larger identifiable groups, such as religious and ethnic minorities and indigenous societies. Cultural rights include a group's ability to preserve its culture, to raise its children in the ways of its ancestors, to continue practicing its language, and not to be deprived of its economic base by the nation-state or large political entity in which it is located.

Cultural Sensitivity - A necessary component of cultural competence, meaning that we make an effort to be aware of the potential and actual cultural factors that affect our interactions with others.

Culture Shock - A state of distress and tension with possible physical symptoms after a person relocates to an unfamiliar cultural environment.

Diaspora - The term was originally used by the ancient Greeks to mean citizens of a large city, who migrated to a conquered land with the purpose of colonization to assimilate the territory into the empire.

Diffusion - The borrowing of cultural traits between societies, either directly or through intermediaries.

Discrimination - Treatment or consideration based on class or category defined by prejudicial attitudes and beliefs rather than individual merit.

Diversity - The concept of diversity means understanding that each individual is unique, and recognizing individual differences along the dimensions of race, ethnicity, gender, sexual orientation, socio-economic status, age, physical abilities, religious beliefs, political beliefs, or other ideologies.

Enculturation - The process whereby an established culture teaches an individual its accepted norms and values, by establishing a context of boundaries and correctness that dictates what is and is not permissible within that society's framework.

Ethnic Competence - The capacity to function effectively in more than one culture, requiring the ability to appreciate and understand features of other ethnic groups and further to interact with people of ethnic groups other than one's own.

Ethnic Group - Group characterized by cultural similarities (shared among members of that group) and differences (between that group and others). Members of an ethnic group share beliefs, values, habits, customs, norms, a common language, religion, history, geography, kinship, and/or race.

Ethnicity - Belonging to a common group with shared heritage, often linked by race, nationality, and language.

Ethnocentrism - Belief in the superiority of one's own ethnic group. Seeing the world through the lenses of one's own people or culture, so that one's own culture always looks best and becomes the pattern everyone else should fit into.

Expatriate - Someone who has left his or her home country to live and work in another country. When we go to another country to live, we become expatriates or expats for short.

Faux Pas - (French word meaning *false step*) A violation of accepted and unwritten, social norms. What is considered good manners in one culture can be considered a faux pas in another.

First Nation - The indigenous population of Canada, excepting the Inuit or **Métis** people.

Individualism - Individualism/Collectivism is one of the Hofstede dimensions in intercultural communication studies. He defines this dimension as: *"individualism pertains to societies in which the ties between individuals are loose: everyone is expected to look after himself or herself and his or her immediate family"* (Hofstede, 1991, p.51).

Integration - The bringing of people of different racial or ethnic groups into unrestricted and equal association, as in society or an organization; desegregation.

Mestizo - A term used to refer to people of partly Native American descent. From Spanish.

Multiracial - The terms multiracial and mixed-race describe people whose parents are not the same race. Multiracial is more commonly used to describe a society or group of people from more than one racial or ethnic group.

Nationalities - Ethnic groups that have, once had, or wish to have or regain, autonomous political status (their own country).

Oreo Cookies - US **racial slur** to refer to a person perceived as black on the outside and white on the inside, hinted by the appearance of an Oreo cookie.

Uncertainty Avoidance - One of the Hofstede dimensions, which he defines as *"the extent to which the members of a culture feel threatened by uncertain or unknown situations"* (Hofstede, 1991).

ADDENDUM

TEN TIPS FOR THE INTERCULTURAL LEADER

Few successful businesses are now mono-cultural in their make-up. Even if a business or organization is not dealing internationally, the chances are that they employ people from foreign countries. At a higher level, globalization has meant companies are looking further afield for new revenue streams, products, services, etc. This requires working and dealing with people from different cultures.

The leaders of today's organizations and businesses need to be adept at managing people of different cultures. They need to be able to grasp the essence of each culture quickly, because culture is so important in shaping customer or employee behavior. Leaders must also learn to shape culture (at least that in their own organizations), so that it is positive and aligned with the direction the organization is taking.

For those looking to the subject and wanting some quick tips on how to improve their intercultural leadership qualities, the following simple tips can get you on your way:

1. Learn about the cultures of people that you work and interact with. Start from scratch and forget your assumptions and stereotypes. There are many free online resources.

2. Read a book about intercultural communication and learn about the subject from an academic level. Noted academics such as Geert Hofstede, Fons Trompenaars, and David Hall have all published books that will go a long way in unraveling the intricacies of cultural differences.

3. Take some formal training from intercultural experts. For little expense, a day course can go a long way in helping you understand how culture impacts you and your work.

4. Try and attend events or occasions where you can immerse yourself in another culture. Use the opportunity to observe how people communicate and interact with one another. If you get the chance to travel abroad, do the same.

5. Start listening and paying more attention when dealing with someone from another culture. You will be surprised how much you pick up by slowing down. Don't jump to conclusions and think actions and behaviors through.

6. Temper your own communication style. Pay attention to the rate at which you speak, what non-verbal messages you may be sending, ask for confirmation of understanding, avoid using slang and idioms.

7. Learn to tolerate uncertainty. There will be a great many unknowns when doing business across cultures. Definitive, concrete answers may not always be given. Focus on what you can determine and try to let go of minor details that are unclear.

8. Be patient with others and yourself. Don't give up. A proper intercultural library of knowledge only comes with time.

9. Keep on top of your own development. Continually assess your advancement and make adjustments.

10. Ask for help and don't be afraid to apologize for mistakes. People generally are appreciative that you are trying to understand them.

The path to effective intercultural leadership is long but not hard. Essentially it is about opening your mind, with which comes greater flexibility and creativity. You will soon see results in your new leadership approach, as you become able to communicate naturally with all manner of cultures in your sphere of work.[89]

Communication Principles

From this experience, we learn the following principles that can help us effectively enter another culture and live peacefully with those in our own cultural context:

1. All of us are products of our cultural heritage, which dictates how we see the world, and how we interact with the world, including gift-giving. Everything we say and do reflects our heritage.

2. We tend to think that everyone else sees and interacts with the world the way we do. Consequently, we become

confused when they do not appreciate our gifts or acts of kindness.
3. Judgment comes quickly: my wife thought I was totally insensitive, and I thought she was an ungrateful snob. We both concluded negative things about the other.
4. When we learn about the other person's cultural heritage, the person's perspective and intentions, we are better able to understand and accept more quickly.
5. Withholding judgment can be the best gift we give to another person, whether spouse, parent, or person from another culture (or within our own culture). This allows us to stay open-minded toward them in order to accomplish the next step.
6. Asking why the other person behaved in a certain way or said something in particular, accomplishes four things:

   - It prompts us to suspend judgment, until all the facts are in.
   - We learn about the other person's cultural heritage, as the other person explains the reasons for feeling/acting in a certain way.
   - We understand how a particular behavior fits into the other's cultural context and becomes a natural way of life for the person.
   - It allows us to change in ways that communicate our true feelings.

However, getting answers can be a bit tricky. Often local people do not know why they do something. Often Westerners do not know why they do certain things, such as elbows off the table or church at 11 o'clock on Sunday morning. Some things become habit, and we have lost the reason for its existence. If you ask a local person why something is done in a certain way, the person may feel defensive, thinking that you are asking a judgmental question. Or the person may feel some shame, if the answer is not known. Ask your questions of local people with whom you have built trust, unless you are asking questions they can answer.[90]

Case Study -- The Dog and the Chickens

A Western missionary came to live in a Two-Thirds World country. Unlike most houses in his neighborhood, his did not have walls. Dogs were not valued in this society, but the missionary, a lover of dogs, had one and furthermore allowed it to run loose.

When the local postmaster told him he was asking people for help, because a neighborhood dog was chasing his chickens at night, the missionary expressed doubt that it was his dog but said he would tie it up at night anyway.

A few days later, the postmaster was much more direct and stern, insisting that the missionary's dog must be tied up at night, because it was still killing his chickens. The missionary had been tying up his dog at night, but sometimes it had gotten loose. When this continued, the missionary found over the next few weeks, that postal workers were obviously cold, no longer giving him prompt help, making him wait longer. The missionary angrily berated them for not doing the jobs they were paid to do.

Eventually, the postmaster openly confronted the missionary telling him he would do something, if the dog kept killing his chickens. That same night, the missionary tied his dog up, but at midnight he heard a shotgun blast from the direction of the post office. Thinking it had nothing to do with him, he went back to sleep. The next morning, his dog was not there, but he decided the dog would turn up later.

When the missionary went to the post office, everyone was very friendly to him, with the postmaster being unusually kind, warmly inquiring about his family, church, and life in general. The Westerner went home, puzzled by this strange change in attitude. Later that night, he realized the shot he had heard the night before was that of his dog being killed after getting itself loose and disturbing the postmaster's chickens. The missionary decided not to make an issue of it and shortly after this, the postmaster became a regular participant in church.[91]

Case Study -- New People, Same Church

Belgrade, Montana is rapidly becoming like Aspen, Colorado—a home, or second home, for folks who can afford to live anywhere.

With fax machines and the Internet, people run international businesses out of their homes. For an area that has traditionally been a ranching community, the culture shock could not be greater.

With the rapid influx of new residents comes a clash of values—not just in the church, but in the community. Newcomers expect the amenities of suburbia. Old-timers complain that people move here to escape the city but bring city problems with them.

The schools are struggling to keep up with enrollment. When we came to Belgrade, they had just built an addition on the middle school. Now they're building again.

Dry Creek Bible Church has shifted its makeup from rural to "rur-ban." We're in a country setting, but of our 120 families, less than 10 make their living from agriculture.

The cost of this influx for the church is that we now have many spiritual rookies, who are young in their faith or don't yet have personal faith in Christ. We can no longer assume people understand church life or grasp basic biblical beliefs. We've also lost some of the family feeling we once had, which used to attract people to us. As we've grown, it's become harder to provide that sense of belonging. And the growth has maxed out our facilities.

What Would You Do?

- What advice would you give the board of this church?
- How could this church of people who do not know each other well create?
- What are the potential benefits of these population shifts for the church?

What Happened

We're constantly reminding people that the mission field is coming to us. I've had people say, "Yeah, that's right. I shouldn't be negative about these people moving in from out of state. I ought to be looking at it as an opportunity." So they're starting to shift their attitude. But it takes a while.

Frankly, most of the fallout has come from newcomers who want the family feeling. Their complaint has been, "We're not appreciated. People don't pay enough attention to us. Our needs aren't being met."

On the other hand, people who used to attend some of the most influential churches in America appreciate our commitment to excellence. They've seen building programs that cost tens of millions, so they don't blink at our $250,000 addition that nearly choked some of our older members!

—Steve Mathewson

Discuss

1. What challenges do we face because of changes in the makeup of our congregation?
2. What message are we currently sending about these changes?
3. How can seeing God at work help to ease the pain of transition (Is. 42: 9–10;
4. Matt. 9:16–17)?

CHAPTER ELEVEN

THE FUTURE OF CULTURAL INTELLIGENCE

Stefan Hankin, president of Lincoln Park Strategies, a Washington-based public opinion research firm stated in 2011 that the future for progressive policies is not about 2012 or the next election in two years. "It's about growing the future and seeing where the path leads us." Hankin may have been postulating on the political implications of racial demographics. He was referring to the fact that within the next 40 years, possibly sooner, the nation will no longer have a majority white population. In a study that his firm released late last year, Hankin noted that the U.S. population will grow by 19 percent over the next two decades, but such growth will not be spread evenly over all racial groups. Whites will increase by almost 4 percent, which pales in comparison to the 63 percent growth rates of Latinos, 55 percent growth of Asians, and the 27 percent increase in the number of blacks. By 2050 the Census Bureau estimates that white Americans will be a statistical minority in the nation, with no racial group comprising more than 50 percent of the population.[92]

This demographic prognosis portends a challenge, not only for those in the political sphere, but its tentacles would be felt across the entire human endeavor. Everything we do in the future would have to include this phenomenon. Whether in business, church, the workplace, school, international trade and commerce, sports, diplomacy, or human resource management, cultural diversity must be factored into the decision making process. And because of this reality, cultural intelligence (CQ) will be a chief cornerstone to building a future in which cultural clashes will not always be a volatile undertaking.

For my denomination, the Church of the Nazarene, unless we have leaders who are culturally intelligent, mistakes would be made that have dangerous implications.

Because of my former responsibility at the Global Ministry Center, I was privy to be actively involved in negotiations with some of the leaders in Ethiopia. The church there was on the verge of entering what would probably have been the greatest missional miracle of the work in Ethiopia. A situation arose that needed the utmost sensitivity to the African Nazarene culture, as empirical evidence would suggest. In my past interaction with the peoples of Africa, as well as the result of sociological research conducted by other scholars, I watched as the American representative leadership missed critical cues to the fast crumbling negotiation.

Gideon Aleyuu (not his real name) had served the Ethiopian church for many years as a much admired leader. In fact I doubt that the denomination would have been in that section of the world without his having favor with the Ethiopian authorities. The end result of the absence of cultural intelligence was a loss of many congregations and the loss of a great leader. True, at the negotiation table were a half dozen Nazarene leaders, all seasoned in the art of diplomacy within their own culture, but again, culture trumped religion, with disastrous results within the Kingdom.

For the foreseeable future, cultural intelligence will emerge as a determining factor in the results we hope to achieve. All indicators in the statistical area show that our tribe is becoming increasingly multicultural, not necessarily by having multicultural congregations, but by having multicultural districts. Some may argue that it is God's desire to have congregations that reflect full diversity, and that ethnic specific congregations are a step towards a truly multicultural church. I have argued that if we are to work for diversity what should be the precursor is a multicultural district. If ethnic churches and pastors cannot be granted full representation and acceptance on predominantly white districts, we might as well give up the ambition to spawn multicultural congregations.

There is hope, however. Hope lies in adopting cultural intelligence as a necessary skill set for all leaders within the denomination and districts. I remember quite well that while serving as national director for Nazarene Compassionate Ministries some were debating what were the skill sets that were necessary to become an effective agency director. While there were those who endorsed a compassionate heart and spiritual sensitivity as necessary, others proposed that business acumen were critically important. So likewise today, cultural intelligence is a must for all leaders. The terrain in which leaders are called upon to lead is defined by demographics.

When asked to describe the "person of tomorrow," Carl Rogers, one of the founders of the field of humanistic psychology, said that in the new world, people will have a desire for creating wholeness in life, thought, and feelings. This "person of tomorrow" will have a need to find and create new experiences that bring a deeper understanding of humanity to work. Similarly, Frances Hasselbein, the former CEO of Girl Scouts, said that people in our societies are looking to find themselves. There is a thirst for personal and inner knowledge and a thirst to understand how this information will uncover a more profound awareness for how we relate to one another.

One day an elephant saw a hummingbird lying flat on its back on the ground; its feet in the air.

"What are you doing," asked the elephant.

The hummingbird replied, "I heard that the sky might fall today. If that happens, I am ready to do my part to hold it up."

The elephant laughed and mocked the bird. "You think those feet can hold up the sky?"

"Not alone," said the bird. "But we must each do what we can, and this is what I can do."[93]

"In today's global marketplace, you must be culturally intelligent. It's a business imperative. America's corporations are becoming more aware of this need. However, they still don't know what to do and how to do it. Instead they supplement a real strategy by supporting <u>diversity</u> associations, donating to non-profit service groups, and increasing their advertising dollars to target the changing faces of their customers. But when it comes to being authentic in how they integrate cultural intelligence into their business model, this is where the executives begin to get uncomfortable."[94]

"Some of the most successful CEOs of our time have demonstrated high cultural intelligence. Think of Carlos Ghosn, born in Brazil, able to turn around an entrenched corporate culture in Japan, and now the CEO of both Nissan and French automaker Renault. He's now such a folk hero in Japan that a comic book has been published chronicling his exploits.

The business world is increasingly international. Companies are increasingly selling goods and sourcing talent from countries like India and China, rather than just manufacturing there.

Investors in the Gulf and elsewhere are increasingly becoming activists and a factor in large mergers.

All of that is going to require CEOs as adept moving across cultures as they are in their home market."[95]

"Cultural Intelligence is the capacity to work effectively with groups of people from any culture. In other words, someone with a high cultural IQ can be dropped in a culture they know nothing about, and they will be able to observe, empathize and be flexible enough to form relationships with people despite not speaking a word of their language. This helps break down biases, and helps people be comfortable in new situations with people from different cultural groups."

Everyone in your organization needs to raise their "cultural IQ" in order to work better together, and be seen as leaders in the global business environment.

When people in organizations or institutions develop a high level of cultural intelligence, they have the skills they need to ask the right questions, give the right answers, and work with people who are from a mixture of different groups in terms of ethnicity, age, religion, economic background, and sexual orientation."[96]

"Companies, too, have cultures, often very distinctive; anyone who joins a new company spends the first few weeks deciphering its cultural code. Within any large company there are sparring subcultures as well: The sales force can't talk to the engineers, and the PR people lose patience with the lawyers. Departments, divisions, professions, geographical regions-each has a constellation of manners, meanings, histories, and values that will confuse the interloper and cause him or her to stumble. Unless, that is, he or she has a high CQ. Cultural intelligence is related to emotional intelligence, but it picks up where emotional intelligence leaves off."[97]

"The ability to interact effectively in multiple cultures is not a skill possessed by all; yet, it is becoming more important in today's global business world. Recently, this skill has been labeled cultural intelligence (CQ), and has caught the attention of business leaders and researchers alike. While previous studies have examined potential outcomes of cultural intelligence, possible antecedents are examined herein. This investigation generates some insight regarding the impact of cultural exposure on CQ, as well as developing an understanding of how the depth of cultural exposure influences a person's cultural intelligence. Findings indicate that certain types of exposures to other cultures (such as education abroad and employment abroad) and the level of exposure from these experiences increases cultural intelligence. These findings are critical for multinational firms as managers hire, promote, train, and prepare employees for international assignments. Additionally, some have discussed how cultural intelligence is a critical skill for global business leaders, and it seems likely that CQ will become increasingly important due to the rise of diversity in the workforce."[98]

"U.S. companies have been trying for decades to capitalize on places like China and India. For many, the progress has been surprisingly slow. The typical approach has been to dump wares on these markets with little thought about how to tailor the products beyond changing the language on the packaging. In contrast, many Asian companies invest significant time improving their cultural intelligence in order to adapt their products and services to the twists and turns of the up and coming global customers.

Millions are expected to join the middle class in emerging markets this year. This doesn't need to be threatening. When pursued with intentionality and cultural intelligence, it can present unprecedented opportunities for your business, wherever you go."[99]

"If a business partner failed to make direct eye contact with you, what conclusions would you make? Would you consider the person dishonest? Lacking in confidence? Scratch your assumptions when you board your flight. In many cultures, including Japan, it is often considered a sign of respect to avoid eye contact. But it doesn't stop there! As a woman, do you think it's polite to cross your legs in a meeting? In Tokyo, make the switch to crossing your ankles instead of your legs and you will avoid upsetting your Japanese colleagues. Since you might not be fluent in the target language, your nonverbal communication skills will become even more crucial. Take some time to study common nonverbal cues in your target country. Doing this could help you establish rapport more quickly with your new partners or clients overseas."[100]

"Many argue that 'the advancement of electronic technology has allowed an increasing number of nations to join the world marketplace, creating diverse and complex global environment that required organization to engage in adaptive strategies in order to remain competitive'. This sounds easier than it actually is. Global market places mean global recognition, meaning each country bringing their unique culture to the forefront and into the corporate, now global, world. Gone are the times when companies would say 'this is the way we do it here'. Leaders of this newly developed Global Corporate World must be aware of the increasingly diverse workforce and 'burgeoning complexity of the social environments within which [the organization] operate[s]'.

An effective global leader must have finely turned awareness of global perspectives, the capacity for recognizing cultural synergies, and the ability to engage in continuous learning. Failure to possess these capacities will result in confusion, frustration, costly failures, and ultimately global corporate failure.[101]

"Our lifestyles are becoming more global and our world is increasingly diverse. This rapid evolution brings greater opportunities for growth, yet most of us underestimate the subtle differences in the way people from diverse backgrounds perceive the world – and how greatly this can impact our success in communicating and doing business with them.

Developing our cultural intelligence can help us interact more effectively with people from all regions of the globe – characterized by different values, customs, attitudes, behaviors, languages, and time zones. If we can effectively perceive how people think, communicate, and behave in cultures different than our own, we will learn to interact with them more successfully."[102]

"Cultural Intelligence is the capacity to work effectively with groups of people from any culture. In other words, someone with a high cultural IQ can be dropped into a culture they know nothing about, and will be able to observe, empathize, and develop relationships with people, despite not speaking a word of their language.

This helps break down biases, prevent incorrect assumptions, and motivate individuals to become comfortable in new situations with people from different cultural groups

Everyone in your organization needs to raise their "cultural IQ" in order to work better together and become leaders in the global business environment.

When people in organizations or institutions develop a high level of cultural intelligence, they have the skills to ask the right questions, give the right answers, and work with people from any culture or cultural mix. (This cultural mix can include ethnicity, age, religion, economic background, sexual orientation, or industry.)"[103]

CQ and the Flat World

In 2005 Thomas Friedman released the first compendium of a candid analysis of the trends in our world, *The World is Flat*. Hardly a book about science, computers, and technology, Friedman reflects on his observation as he visited countries based in China and India. What he discovered through these visits was a giant exodus of jobs from the US. What fascinated Friedman was the ease and rapidity with which call centers were being set up in these countries by Western companies like Dell, AOL, and Microsoft. From my first reading of Friedman's text, I have concluded that the book failed to accept the inevitability of the flattened world, and sought to offer advice to the American business community on how to make the Western workplace more employee-friendly.

Friedman's advice was indeed pathological, offering formulas for unscrambling the egg of business, commerce, and globalization. What is necessary, in my humble opinion, in a flattened world is not a reversal of the trend, but the optimization of the capacity of individuals to compete effectively, smartly, and efficiently in alien cultures. Cultural intelligence must emerge as a mandatory skill set of human resource persons. Employees and organizations that are guided by the acknowledgment of the need for a global identity will flourish in this new flattened environment.

I believe that CQ motivation would facilitate a relational reciprocity that brings a competitive advantage to both host country and the sending countries. Individuals who recognize the contribution that CQ brings to the workplace will facilitate the business edge by enabling a broad range of perspectives, skills, and insights which would result in mitigating conflict and misunderstanding.

Prior to Friedman's pronouncement, Americans traveled primarily for three reasons – volunteer work, study, and military assignments. What however has surfaced in the past decade is travel for *business purposes*, where the bottom line or the motivating factor shifted significantly. Obviously, there were economically feasible reasons for these business arrangements. Firstly, there was a lack of local talent and expertise present when companies elected to move their operations overseas. Secondly, it became necessary to transfer technical expertise, technology, standard operating procedures, and organizational routines to the host country. Thirdly, host-country managers had to be developed with a global mindset. And fourthly, it was important that host-country possess parent-country orientation.[104] Removed from their familiar cultural settings wherein daily living habits were well known, these new leaders experienced constant frustration and occupational stress. In these situations, culture trumped business protocols and strategy.

Likewise, for those of us who are engaged in evangelism and church growth among different people groups, cultural intelligence is indispensable, and will be the essential tool for future ministry. It is like American Express, don't leave home without it. If we count the cost of not doing ministry with a handle on cultural intelligence, it is staggering. Since however, at the writing of this book I don't have the figures for failures in cross-cultural Christian ministry, I will have to be content on citing the effects in the global workplace when CQ is not appropriated properly, or for that matter, given top priority. According to researchers Randall Schuler and Peter Dowling, reports of U.S. expatriates who fail to complete their assignments because of a lack of CQ is about 15 percent, while for companies in Europe and Japan it is about 8 to 10 percent. For these companies, the cost of failures include paying for travel for the expat and his or her family, shipping their belongings overseas, managing housing and property, insurance, and return to home expenditures. The estimated cost per failure is in the range of US$250,000 to $1 million depending on the specifics of the expat's assignment. It gets even worse. There is additional cost because of the disruption and displacement of the worker from the home base, since the selected worker is usually a highly successful and productive person.

These afore-mentioned estimates should bring a sober pause for those who are engaged in the most important mission on earth. I am sure that the degree of loss would depend largely on the cultural distances between people groups. But regardless, the price paid for a lack of cultural intelligence is always too high.

When I served as director for multicultural ministries in our denomination's headquarters there were many conversations with district superintendents about leaders from different people groups. Very often, it was my conclusion that the host culture failed to acknowledge that there was a fundamental difference in the definition of the role of leadership. No one will argue that the failure or success of any endeavor rises or falls on leadership. But how do we define leadership? Is the definition of leadership the same in every culture? If it isn't, and I would argue that it isn't, then the expectations from these leaders could be sadly and wrongfully analyzed.

Leaders from every culture are aware of the characteristics of leadership as defined within their own culture. When working within that culture it is not difficult to evaluate success by the standards that are established as markers established by that culture. It follows then, that when working in another culture it is imperative that the behaviors and styles of perceived successful leaders within that other culture be acknowledged and appreciated. The future of CQ is embedded within this imperative.

Last week I traveled to Antigua to speak at an annual conference organized by four different Christian organizations. It was readily acknowledged that each of these organizations differed in their theological definitions of evangelism and discipleship. The greater challenge however, was that each of the leaders of these organizations represented a different island, not Antigua. I witnessed the exercise of each island representative expressing values that clearly were important to them because of their understanding of leadership. This conference was a success because these leaders were culturally intelligent, at least to the degree that they understood the individual's interpretation of leadership. The future of CQ and CQ training was demonstrated by the manner in which consensus was achieved within the team.

The success or failure of any initiative may very well rest on being culturally aware. We will be bound together by long held convictions about our creedal beliefs, but CQ will emerge as the dominant capability.

Very often, the business and corporate world would set the pace for the religious world. Wal-Mart is not one of my favorite stores, particularly because I have strong objections to their position on labor representation, vis-à-vis the trade unions. Additionally, I have spoken before of their policies that reflect a less than favorable attitude towards gender equity. However, an article in 2009 about the expansion of their markets within cultural groups tells the story succinctly about the future of CQ:

Wal-Mart plans to open its first Hispanic-focused supermarkets this summer in Arizona and Texas as the largest US retailer continues its drive to expand its dominance of the US grocery business.

The pilot stores, named Supermercado de Walmart, will open in Phoenix and Houston in remodeled 39,000 sq ft locations occupied previously by two of Wal-Mart's Neighborhood Market stores.

The retailer said that the stores were in "strongly Hispanic neighborhoods" and would feature a "new lay-out, signing and product assortment designed to make them even more relevant to local Hispanic customers". The staff will also be bilingual.

Wal-Mart's Sam's Club warehouse store also plans to open a 143,000 sq ft Hispanic-focused store called Más Club in Houston this year.

Several leading regional US supermarket chains already operate Hispanic store brands, including Publix in Florida, which operates three Publix Sabor markets, and HEB in Texas, which opened a Mi Tienda store in Houston in 2006.

The markets include elements such as cafés serving Latino pastries and coffee, and full service meat and fish counters.

Leading retailers are also pursuing Hispanic consumers online, with Best Buy and Home Depot having launched Spanish-language versions of their e-commerce sites in recent months.

Eduardo Castro-Wright, the head of Wal-Mart's US stores since 2005, has also been an advocate of testing new smaller, more focused formats, and raised the idea of turning the Neighborhood Market into a Hispanic-style bodega concept several years ago.

He has also developed Wal-Mart's efforts to customize its larger Supercenter stores, which have been grouped according to differing community profiles, such as urban, suburban, Hispanic and African-American, with customized merchandise.

A 195,000 sq ft Supercenter that opened in Texas last year included a tortilleria bakery, Hispanic foods and a larger selection of Spanish-language music and DVDs.

Mr. Castro-Wright was previously head of Wal-Mart's Mexican subsidiary, whose store network ranges from large US-style Supercenters to small local bodegas, an upmarket supermarket chain and two restaurant chains.

Last year, Wal-Mart also began testing four new 10,000 sq ft Marketside convenience grocery stores in the Phoenix area – its first new format in a decade. Tesco, the UK retailer, also has more than 25 of its small Fresh & Easy markets in the Phoenix area.[105]

Culture trumped strategy for Wal-Mart in the same way that culture trumps religion. For Wal-Mart, to have ignored the signs of the times would have spelt economic disaster resulting from missed opportunities. For the church, if culture is not given its rightful place, we will miss the divinely appointed opportunities for church growth and missionary revitalization.

CHAPTER TWELVE

ON BECOMING CULTURALLY INTELLIGENT

"You see, your problem is that you keep thinking in English, and then you pursue the arduous task of translating into Spanish. You lose too much time in translation, and the essence of what is intended is lost!"

Could Dave really be correct? It seemed so primordial an answer. There must be something more complicated than that. Dave is my younger brother, and he accompanied me on a trip a few months ago to Costa Rica, where I was fulfilling a request to speak at the Holiness Summit held at the seminary.

As is always the case when I am in the Latin culture, I was enthralled and mystified by the Spanish language. There is something utterly romantic and soul-gripping about being immersed in a group of Spanish-speaking Nazarenes. Every time I experience it, I come away with a sanctified resolve to learn or to at least to acquire a working knowledge of the language in preparation for my ultimate sojourn to heaven because, as is so often repeated, Spanish is the language of the angels.

Dave, sensing my yearning to one day speak the language, or at least to be functionally conversational, gave me the sagacious advice to "think in Spanish!" I have begun that journey, and as much as I hate to admit it, my younger brother was right. (In my culture, he's not supposed to be!)

Essentially, the same holds true if one is to master the journey to thinking cross-culturally. Thinking cross-culturally is to experience the incarnation all over again. It is the art of thinking in the context of the people you are committed to reaching with the message of the Gospel or the Good News. However, one cannot think cross-culturally unless one takes the time and puts in the effort to study the language, tradition, history, values, assumptions, and customs of the culture. To do otherwise is to invite frustration and failure and, more to the point, to risk the automatic reaction of blaming the people of the other culture for not being willing to accede to our way of doing things, of insisting that our worldview must take precedence over theirs.

The age-old debate about Christ's role in transforming culture will forever continue. More than fifty years after H. Richard Niebuhr's epic text *Christ and Culture*, theologians and missionaries are still seriously engulfed in the discussion. Time and space will not allow me to deal here with the five-fold taxonomies and typology advanced by the Niebuhrian followers over the half a century since he made his proposition but, for whatever it's worth as a contribution to the thesis of cross-cultural thinking that I propose, I will make a broad statement here: The difficulty with Niebuhr's position is that it allows a Christological deficiency that views culture as both the villain and the protagonist, but culture is not inherently and intrinsically evil. Aspects of culture might not be desirable for living out the life of discipleship for the ardent follower of Christ, but these aspects of culture should not be the determinants in the relationship between Christ and culture.

It is no secret that Christianity always bears the imprint of the socio-cultural milieu in which it exists. As such, culture should not be considered a liability from which Christianity needs to be rescued. Sadly, throughout history it seems that the task of the Church has been to subjugate culture because leaders of the church have advocated that this is the only way to preserve the integrity of Christianity from cultural taint. However, the truth is that Christianity cannot be an effective witness of its relevance without mediation. That mediation could be found in the revelation that God's self exists in all cultures. Further mediation could be discovered in the fact that culture and the Christian faith can coexist only because of the intentional interaction between them. In fact, Merci Amba Oduyoye might have been on to something sublime when she stated that "Christian theology can be aided by African religious beliefs and practices."[106]

The position I now propose we undertake in an effort to become effective cross-cultural emissaries in a pluralistic world, where culture will not go away, is that the task of the church should not be to Christianize culture but to allow culture to "culturize" the Gospel. This reversal in thinking may help restore the respect that all culture deserves and for which it has been petitioning. As this chapter will propose, culture is the indispensable soil for the propagation of the Gospel, and we must not fear that the "culturalization" of the Gospel will condense its message or blunt its efficacy. Rather, the accommodation of culture may help to restore the authenticity and integrity of the message.

So let's all take a step back and explore what it means to think cross-culturally.

Undoubtedly, there is no greater cross-cultural thinker than Jesus. His journey from the portals of heavenly ecstasy to incarnation was the result of cross-cultural thinking. The more one exegetes the incarnation, the more unthinkable it becomes to lose sight of the reality that LOVE for the Other is the cornerstone of cross-cultural thinking. Follow Jesus on his interaction with humanity while He lived here on earth, and that conclusion can defend itself. What Jesus demonstrated for us to witness was a lesson in cultural intelligence.

Our Cultural intelligence Quotient (CQ) is the level of our ability to function effectively in a variety of cultural contexts, including national, ethnic, organizational, generational, and many other contexts. To think cross-culturally is to become a student of cultural intelligence. True disciples of Jesus will consciously seek to be culturally intelligent so that ministry across cultures can be wholesome. The times in which we live demand that we become culturally adept in thinking cross-culturally. The heralded practitioners of cross-cultural thinking have been missionaries who, for centuries, have perfected the art and science of this discipline, but the discipline has been grounded in a pedagogical research approach through anthropology and sociology. On the other hand, CQ is a relatively new model grounded in the fields of anthropology, sociology, and psychology as well as experiential research from the fields of business, education, and missions. As a consequence, CQ thinking is transformed into a meta-model.

What makes a meta-model different? Ordinarily, when faced with a cross-cultural assignment, we pursue a learning path that focuses for the most part on the cultural values and assumptions of a people and how one can relate to that culture. However, CQ collects data in order to allow it to inform the manner in which interaction is managed, particularly as it relates to behavior. This is not as complicated as it first appears. We are all acquainted with IQ, which is an indicator of our intellectual intelligence, and EQ, which is a measurement of how we handle our emotions in difficult situations. CQ is a useful, coherent framework that accounts for our internal and external dynamics as we encounter cross-cultural situations. It is a measurement of our capacity to move seamlessly in and out of unfamiliar cultural venues. Hence, CQ takes up where IQ and EQ left off.

Thinking cross-culturally is fundamentally the deployment of the cognitive and meta-cognitive facilities of the mind. Such thinking can be either utterly frustrating or graciously rewarding. With the plethora of cultural challenges before us, the ability to multi-task culturally is no liability. Cultural challenges face us in three fundamental areas of human engagement: socio-ethnic, generational, and organizational. Of course, each of these categories could be further subdivided into subsets, and the subsets into sub-subset, but this chapter focuses on the socio-ethnic area of human engagement in order to expose the need for right thinking and to suggest a research-tested path to the enhancement of CQ. CQ is the recommended tool for enhancing strategies to adapt in a multicultural environment, to think cross-culturally.

Philip Jenkins staggered the Christian world with his candid assessment of the trends that he believed were imminent and that would affect the future of Christianity. In his book, *The Next Christendom: The Coming of the Global Church,* Jenkins posited that we are living in the most transforming times in the history of the church. Old missiological paradigms are being shifted, long-held traditions are being questioned, communication strategies are being assessed and evaluated, and mission and vision are being realigned to meet the demands of a new world order. For more than two centuries the Western worldview has been inextricably woven into the fabric of the Christian church. Western values and cultural constructs have, whether intentionally or not, framed the context for the church, but Jenkins breaks the news that the center of the church is being aggressively pulled from its assumed safe moorings in the West (Europe and North America) toward the South, that is, Africa, Asia, and Latin America. As Kenyan scholar John Mbiti stated, "The centers of the church's universality [are] no longer in Geneva, Rome, Athens, Paris, London, New York, but Kinshasa, Buenos Aires, Addis Ababa and Manila."[107]

According to the *World Christian Encyclopedia*, the trend of the future growth of Christianity cannot be business as usual! With the world population of Christians at 2.1 billion, the largest single

Christian population bloc—Europe, with 570 million—is now closely rivaled by Latin America with 490 million, Africa with 370 million, and Asia with 323 million. North America claims "only" 260 million believers. Extrapolating these figures to 2025, there will be around 2.6 billion Christians, of whom 633 million will live in Africa, 640 million in Latin America, and 460 million in Asia. Europe, with 555 million, will have slipped to third place.[108]

Even more telling is that:

- An average of 178,000 persons are converted daily.
- An average of 35,000 conversions occur each day in Latin America.
- Latin America was home to only 50,000 Christians in 1900. By 1980 there were more than 20 million, and in 2010, there are over 480 million.
- In China, an average of 28,000 conversions occur each day. When China became closed to Christianity in 1950, there were a million Christians. Today's estimates are nearing 100 million.
- In 1900, Korea was deemed impossible to penetrate with the gospel. Now South Korea is reported to be more than 40% Christian, with more than 7,000 churches in Seoul alone.
- More people have been converted in Iran in the past 10 years than in the previous 2,000 years combined.
- An average of 20,000 conversions occur in Africa each day. Forty percent of Africa is said to be Christian.
- None of the 50 largest churches in the world are found in North America. In Seoul, there are 253,000 members in the Yoido Full Gospel Church.
- With a 6.9% growth rate, Christianity is the fastest-growing religion in the world, compared to a growth rate of 2.7% for Muslims, 2.2% for Hindus, and 1.7% for Buddhists.

Putting CQ to work in thinking cross-culturally.

In light of these drastic, world-changing phenomena, how should leaders react? How should we put CQ to work? In order to appreciate the contribution of CQ fully in this important task of thinking cross-culturally, it is necessary to delve farther into the research upon which CQ is based. Two areas are of particular interest to us in understanding the potential for using CQ as an effective instrument in thinking cross-culturally: the research and historical background of CQ, and a toolkit for improving our CQ.

Research and Historical Background

P. Christopher Early, Ph.D., a renowned scholar in organizational behavior principles focusing on cross-cultural issues, work motivation and the cognitive processes underlying individual actions, and Soon Ang, Goh Tjoei Kok Chair Professor in International Management & IT at the Nanyang Business School, Nanyang Technological University, Singapore, introduced the concept of CQ in their Stanford University Press book published in 2003.[109] The driving query behind the discovery was: *Why do some, but not other, individuals easily and effectively adapt their views and behaviors cross-culturally?* Since then, despite being such a new discipline, CQ has been mentioned in over 60 journals "in disciplines as diverse as applied, cognitive, and social psychology, mental health, international business, management, organizational behavior, human resources, human relations, industrial relations, intercultural relations, sociology, education, communications, knowledge management, decision science, military, architecture, economics, and engineering."[110]

The core concept of CQ was built on the four-factor model of intelligence: cognition, meta-cognition, motivation, and behavior. Earley and Ang contended that meta-cognitive, cognitive, and motivational intelligence involve mental functioning but that behavioral intelligence is the ability to display behaviors that enhance the cross-cultural experience.

Metacognitive CQ.

Persons who have a high metacognitive CQ have a keen sense of their cross-cultural surroundings and are able to adjust easily as new knowledge about prior assumptions makes clear the need to adapt. Ever so often, one discovers that assumptions were misplaced, but if changes in interactions are not put into practice as a result of the discovery, the exercise would end in disaster. The understanding that changes must be made empowers the cross-cultural worker to release himself or herself from reliance on old assumptions. High metacognitive CQ opens the door for the inflow of new strategic thinking or heuristics that enable us to move forward to the accomplishment of the planned mission.

Metacognitive CQ is indispensible for three reasons: a) it promotes active cross-cultural thinking about persons and situations; b) it triggers active challenges to unyielding dependence on culture-bound thinking; and c) it encourages people to revise and adapt strategies.

Cognitive CQ.

Cognitive CQ is the knowledge about the norms, patterns, universals, and conventions in new cultures that can help to guide our engagement. In the latter section of this chapter, which addresses the cultural toolkits, we will talk about the manner in which cultures develop indigenous values that shape people's behavior. When cognitive CQ is allowed to stand alone as the sole determinant of behavior, it can be very misleading because cognitive knowledge of the culture does not take into consideration the underlying history and values that have led to what can be seen of that culture.

The thoughts and actions of a particular culture are shaped by invisible systems operative beneath the surface, and it is incumbent on the one studying the culture to be aware of them.

Motivational CQ.

Herein lies the LOVE element to which I alluded earlier. Motivational CQ is critically important because, when frustration sets in, it is our motivation that keeps us going. Motivation compels us to seek adequate knowledge of the new culture and to preserve the vision that stimulated the decision to learn about the culture in the first place. The expectancy-value theory of motivation (Eccles & Wigfield, 2002) states that "the direction and magnitude of energy channeled toward a particular task involve two elements – the expectation of successfully accomplishing the task and the value associated with accomplishing the task. Those with high motivational CQ direct attention and energy toward cross-cultural situations based on interest (Deci & Ryan, 1895) and confidence in cross-cultural effectiveness (Bandura, 2002)."[111]

Behavioral CQ.

Behavioral CQ is reflective of one's potential to exhibit suitable behavior verbally and non-verbally. Those with high behavioral CQ are flexible and easily assess the cues about what is and isn't appropriate in terms of behavior. When one works in foreign countries, appropriate behavior patterns may not be readily revealed, and it is only by a close study of non-verbal actions that flexibility could be exercised.

Often, it is difficult in face-to-face interactions to access the latent thoughts that another communicates non-verbally; but a person with a high Behavioral CQ will have an easier time reading cues.

Toolkit for Improving CQ

Cross-cultural leaders with high CQs understand how to encounter new cultural situations, judge what goes on in them and make appropriate adjustments to behave effectively in those otherwise disorienting circumstances. They have repertoires of strategies and behaviors for orienting themselves when they encounter unfamiliar behaviors and perspectives so they can discern whether an unfamiliar behavior is explained by culture or is unique to a particular person or group. Such discernment is critical in, for instance, sponsoring new congregations, understanding new cultural opportunities, unifying dispersed leadership teams, and developing strategic plans for missions.

The four factors of CQ—metacognition, cognition, motivation, and behavior—can be further expanded in terms of how one enhances one's CQ. The work of missions has given considerable attention to Motivational CQ and Behavioral CQ but has not been as eager to address Cognitive and Metacognitive CQ. Why is this so? The Christian missionary enterprise has a ready-made motivation for engagement in mission enterprise, particularly in short-term mission trips, and the Great Commission and the Great Commandment serve as the pattern for motivation. As for behavior, it is commonly believed that, with the introduction of the Christ message, many groups will be more accepting of the expat's behavioral patterns. As a result, although they are the most talked about, Motivational CQ and Behavioral CQ seem to need the least attention, so we'll spend more time on Cognitive CQ and Metacognitive CQ.

Let me unpack these factors in greater detail.

CQ DRIVE (MOTIVATION)

Effective cross-cultural thinking goes beyond the collection of knowledge about a particular culture and beyond merely understanding what is happening with the one with whom one is interacting. CQ Drive has more to do with the mental conditioning necessary to pursue a cross-cultural assignment when things don't seem to be going right. What is it about the assignment that will motivate us to persevere? Answering informal set of questions can help us to be honest with ourselves:

- Do I like cross-cultural interactions that are new to me?
- Do I prefer to stay with locals when I travel cross-culturally, rather than in a hotel by myself?
- Do I prefer eating local foods when I go to a new place?
- Do I enjoy spending time with people who don't embrace Christianity as their worldview?
- Am I confident I would be effective in cross-cultural ministry?[112]

When these kinds of questions are honestly answered, we can discover our level of self-efficacy. Self-efficacy is an important gauge of one's CQ Drive because it tells whether one is really up to the challenge since "without a strong sense of self efficacy, a person will avoid challenges and give up easily when confronted with setbacks. The motivational aspect of cultural intelligence requires a personal sense of efficacy and desire for enactive mastery."[113] This art is sometimes referred to as "anticipatory socialization" or the ability to be constantly in tune with what it will take to continue on a journey that is so fraught with dismay and failure. Often the journey is aborted because the traveler spent insufficient time considering the acute differences in the other culture. The manner in which one anticipates all the surprises that could surface will determine one's capacity to adjust to the changing environment because that capacity is the key factor in cross-cultural thinking and modification.

Culture shock in a new situation also can serve to derail cross-cultural ministry, especially if the experience is a negative or unpleasant one. How does one continue? This period of disorientation can be effectively mitigated by revisiting all or parts of the assumptions and behaviors that we had previously taken for granted. In summary, here are the pointers that can help one improve CQ Drive in cross-cultural thinking and the experience of ministry:

- Be honest with yourself. Be aware of the challenges that surface, and take inventory of the discomfort you are experiencing.

- Examine your confidence level. Do you have enough confidence that you can be successful and fruitful in this assignment if you continue?

- Eat and socialize. Share meals in both formal and informal settings. It takes a lot of motivation to eat unfamiliar foods, but learning to like some of those foods can be if value, even if your prayer is "Dear God, help me to keep it down!"

- Count the perks. Don't take the collateral benefits that are serendipitously revealed on the journey for granted, as they serve as excellent motivators for a weary traveler.

- Become passionate about the bottom line. The challenge for all who become involved in cross-cultural thinking is to be anchored to the bottom line. What difference would it make if you fail in this assignment? What difference would it make if you succeed?

Key Question: What's your level of confidence and motivation for this cross-cultural assignment? If it's lacking, what can you do to increase it?

For successful adaptation to a new culture, a person must be sufficiently motivated to want to associate with those who are part of that culture and be more than willing to go the extra mile in seeking opportunities for meaningful interaction. It is not sufficient to know why young male Nazarene pastors hold hands in Ethiopia; one must also be motivated to adapt and adjust to the culture.

CQ KNOWLEDGE (COGNITION)

The single most powerful word in cross-cultural thinking is "UNDERSTAND." Cognition CQ is the quest to understand what culture is and how it shapes us. To miss this important and salient point is to court disaster and invite failure. Here are some initial questions that can reveal whether we currently have the driving force to acquire more knowledge about cultures other than our own and what we must do to acquire it:

- Am I fluent in a language other than English?
- Do I know the ways other cultures approach conflict? Do I know the different role expectations of men and women in other cultures?
- Do I know the basic cultural values of several cultures?
- Do I understand the primary ways Christians differ in their beliefs and practices in different cultural settings?[114]

(In my view, CQ Knowledge and CQ Strategy are the most important factors in improving one's cross-cultural thinking. They complement each other because they hold each other accountable.)

The first step in understanding cultural differences is to understand one's own culture. Ignoring the need to understand one's own culture—or assuming one has already mastered it simply because one has lived in the culture for decades—is probably just as disastrous as ignoring the shades and nuances of another culture. An educated contrast between one's own culture and that of another will take effort, energy, and inquisitiveness. American culture, after all, is not a monolith: consider the difficult task of defining the "average American." Learning everything about one's own culture will take a lifetime, so maybe the approach we should take is to come up with appropriate handles to define what culture is, and what it is not.

<u>Going below the surface</u>

How often do we hear well meaning, zealous Christians say, "People are people. Sin is sin. Jesus is Jesus"? This attitude demonstrates a lack of appreciation for the impact that culture has on its people. In discussions with our pastors and leaders as I travel around the country, it's simply amazing how uninformed people are about the significance of culture. The idealistic dream proposed by Israel Zangwill that America is a melting pot has not served us well in this regard. My reaction to those proponents has always been that America was never a melting pot and will never be a melting pot; instead, it is more like a salad bowl, in which all the ingredients retain their individual shapes, but add significantly to the whole, and which are pungently blended by the salad dressing, which is the loyalty to the common denominator, Christ.

The attempt to define culture is very much like defining air. Although we can't see it, we know it's there. We feel its effects. We benefit from an abundant supply. Air shapes how we live, and culture works in similar fashion: its tentacles dig deeply into a society and colonize its citizens indiscriminately. The task before us now is to view some of the salient features of culture and its mystifying effects upon all within its reach. Thinking cross-culturally is to enter this journey.

Some definitions of culture may be helpful at this point:

- Culture is the artificial, secondary environment superimposed on the natural.[115]
- Culture is "a pattern of thinking, feeling, and reacting to various situations and actions."[116]
- Culture is the shared understandings people use within a society to align their actions. "While culture is defined, created, and transmitted through interaction, it is not interaction itself, but the content, meanings, and topics of interaction."[117]

- Culture is the collective programming of the mind that distinguishes the members of one group from another. It is the software behind how we operate.[118]
- Culture is the way a group of people solve problems and reconcile dilemmas.[119]
- Cultures are comprised of "webs of significance" that people spin and in which they themselves are suspended.[120]

There is probably no more vivid a metaphor that gives the reader a real sense of culture than that of the iceberg. As is shown in Figure 1, what are visible to those who want to know about a culture are its artifacts and effects, like the gestures and habits, music, economic practices, dress, use of physical space, order of worship, and choice of liturgy. However, like the iceberg, the most critical components that make and shape culture are not visible but are submerged beneath the surface.

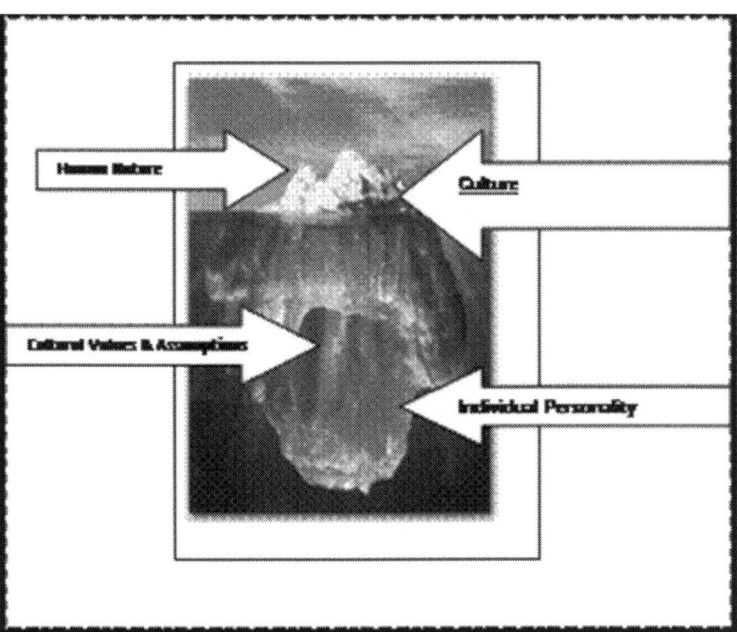

A sure way to exegete another's culture is to undertake a careful study of the cultural values that seem to be present in all cultures. These five values stem from the long-standing literature on how people from every culture deal with their environments.

Individual Cultural Value Orientations

Individual cultural value orientations represent the emphasis or the value that an individual places on a specific aspect of culture. Individual cultural values are influenced by national cultural values and are learned during early socialization. Although those with similar cultural backgrounds tend to have similar cultural values, there is variability in cultural values in all groups and within all organizations.

Please note as we review these cultural values that they reflect only an individual's personal emphasis and preferences. Being "low" or "high" on a specific cultural value has no built-in meaning; it is not "better" to be low or high. Individual cultural value orientations are simply descriptions of preferences. Event Time vs. Clock Time – In cultures that focus on event time, events begin and end when all the participants feel the time is right, rather than artificially imposing clock time. This value is probably the cause of most misunderstandings among immigrant cultures in the US and Canada. Clock time is a precious commodity in developed industrial countries where punctuality and strict adherence to a schedule is important, but event time is the accepted modus operandi in developing countries, where relationships take precedence over schedules. When working with groups from other countries, one should pay close attention to these clues.

In organizational structures understanding this orientation toward time is important because the organization's time orientation contributes to its focus on the past, present, or future. Generational wars are fermented within this lack of knowledge. I am witness to the fact that most Anglo congregations who give worship space to an group from another culture are sometimes not sensitive about this area, as the other culture may or may not take up exactly the 10 minutes (or 15 or 5) they're given in the order of service. As a naturalized American citizen from another culture, I have never really understood Americans' infatuation with time, although I have come to appreciate the consistency. Sadly, most Americans believe that "punctuality is a virtue and have never thought about other ways of being on time, other than noting 'clock time'."[121]

High Context vs. Low Context – In high-context cultures, people have significant history together, so a great deal of mutual understanding can be assumed. In high-context cultures, communication is indirect and emphasizes implicit roles and understanding. A low-context culture is one in which, because there is not a long, detailed history of existence together, much attention is placed on communication and nothing is left to a guessing game.

How we behave in church services on Sunday mornings is an example of high context at work in a negative way. For the most part, it is assumed that the "church family" knows the rules and protocols for behavior, but when a visitor enters the building, she is in a strange land without clues or signs because the members assume that everyone knows how to behave and knows the difference between the Old and New Testaments. Notice how often Scripture is cited in sermons with chapter and verse, as though the visitors understand the references. The church of today exists in a very high context, and we wonder why visitors never return.

An effort to enhance one's CQ Knowledge should involve the study of the context in which cultures exist.

Individualism vs. Collectivism -- Some cultures are largely governed by a commitment to do what's best for the individual. Studies have shown that the US scores higher than any other nation in individualism, with Australia, the United Kingdom, Canada, and the Netherlands close behind. People from individualistic cultures treasure self-reliance and tend to retain functional, relatively tenuous bonds with others. On the other end of the continuum is China, which scored the highest in collectivism. In collectivist cultures, the needs of the group are more important than the needs of the individual, so collectivist cultures emphasize families, work groups, communities and other groups above the individual. Most Asian cultures are collectivist, as are most Latin American and African cultures.

Church-planters should garner information about immigrant groups so expectations can be based on the group's cultural orientation in terms of individualism and collectivism. Many missionaries working in collectivistic cultures become frustrated because members are reluctant to engage personal accountability and initiative. The point to remember is that *individualism orientation* emphasizes "I" and individual identity and prefers individual decisions and working alone, while *collectivism orientation* emphasizes "We" and group identity and prefers group decisions and working with others.

<u>Low vs. High Power Distance</u> – A narrative account of low vs. high power is probably the best way to tell this story. American manager John Potts operates a maquiladora just inside Arizona's border with Mexico. His American employees have always considered him to be sympathetic and sensitive to their needs. As a way to get to know his Mexican workforce better, Potts arranged a dinner at his house and invited three of his Mexican managers. After refusing the invitation several times, the managers agreed to take him up on the offer. From his perspective, the dinner went well, and he felt that the experience opened new doors of communication.

One week after the dinner two of the managers quit. Potts was disheartened. What signals had he missed? What might he have said that offended the managers? What protocols did he violate in inviting them to his home? What was it about the food that he and his wife served?

Later, Potts learned that it was nothing that he had said. However, the dinner lowered the power distance between him and these managers; the act of socializing with them ran counter to the cultural work environment, and the managers feared that they might be expected to do the same with their workers, and that doing so would make it difficult for them to demand the respect and loyalty from them that they felt they deserved. Removal of the power distance was alien to the men's culture, and Potts' invitation destroyed an element that was an essential tool for effective management in that culture. While he was seen as an empathetic boss in his own culture, in the Mexican managers' culture, he was seen as weak. He missed the cues that should have alerted him of these significant differences.

<u>Low vs. High Uncertainty Avoidance</u> – Uncertainty avoidance is the extent to which the culture feels comfortable with risk. *Low Uncertainty Avoidance cultures* prefer few rules, less structure,

and fewer guidelines and tolerate unstructured and unpredictable situations well. *High Uncertainty Avoidance cultures* prefer written rules, structure, and guidelines and are uncomfortable with unstructured or unpredictable situations. Research has shown that Britain, Jamaica, and Sweden lead the way in low uncertainty. Those of us from the Caribbean would attest to the reality that Jamaicans are, by and large, an expeditious and risk-taking people.

Thinking cross-culturally means paying attention to a culture's attitude toward risk, for it will determine the level of detail at which a strategy should be communicated.

Key Question: What cultural understanding do you need for this cross-cultural assignment?

CQ STRATEGY (METACOGNITION)

Thinking cross-culturally involves not only the collection of knowledge about another culture, but also a strategy of engagement for the interaction. Determining a strategy of engagement is a little like deciding whether to use the cruise control when one drives. When one is driving in a familiar environment, it may be advisable and wise to use the cruise control because there is little need to negotiate unfamiliar terrain. However, driving in an unfamiliar environment requires a different set of skills, including being acutely aware of the intersections, signs, pedestrians, and signals. Under these circumstances, one would not be advised to use cruise control.

Similarly, shutting down some of our "automatic" behavior when we are in a new context allows us to be more aware of the cues from the environment and to recognize the opportunity to change our previous knowledge or assumptions based on what is actually happening. However, awareness of the environment may not be sufficient; it is also important to be self-aware. What is happening to you while you are encountering this new activity? How comfortable are you? Which of your assumptions are being challenged? Cross-cultural thinking demands assessment of the situation and is indispensable to effectiveness in ministry.

As a frequent speaker in churches with members from other cultures, I have often found myself in a situation where it is easy to ignore the cultural setting in which the sermon is being presented. Preaching to a Black audience is different from preaching to people from any other culture. The call and response genre that is an interactive cue within Black congregations and that may incite a continuous sense of movement and crescendo may be absent in other congregations. To ignore the difference in the culture of the group for which the sermon is being preached could ruin an opportunity to bring good tidings to weary travelers. It is hard enough to preach in a familiar setting; without intentional awareness in an unfamiliar one, one's efforts are likely to be futile.

When I am asked to present a workshop in an unfamiliar church, community, or state, I try to be keenly aware of the room, its decorations, the seating arrangement, the noises, the paint on the walls, how the participants are dressed, and the books or literature on display. As time goes on, I take note of my assumptions that are incorrect so I can adapt and adjust to the reality. This is where I must answer the *why* question of the new situation: why is it as it is? To answer this question, I must be aware so my initial interpretation, which may be way off base, does not derail my effort and goal. In familiar settings this process is easy, but in unfamiliar settings our thinking skills must be heightened.

Becoming aware is an active thinking process of gleaning the understanding gained from a preliminary assessment of the culture to which we are being called to minister. How often, when one is placed in a new environment, does one discover that one's initial observations clashed with later interpretation of that environment? Effective cultural thinking mitigates the damage that could be the result of such variations.

Recently, leaders have become interested in Strengths Finder and a host of other profile and strength assessments. These resources can be helpful in our cross-cultural thinking. For example, my top strength on the Gallup Strengths Finder is "input," which is a characteristic of one who enjoys collecting information even without any immediate purpose in mind. I find the world interesting merely because of its infinite variety and complexity, and collecting data keeps my mind fresh, always cognizant that I have at my disposal a ready reservoir of information stored away for future use. However, as I interact with others in different contexts, I must be aware of this trait and consider the impact it may have on others who are not similarly inclined. To those who are not of my particular intellectual persuasion, frustration can ensue when I indulge in communicating some arcane bit of knowledge I've picked up, and my efforts can be misconstrued as "showing off" or as elitism, or at best as a total waste of time. As we become aware of how our own behavior is perceived, we can begin to maneuver within the context to achieve the results we want.

The real challenge of developing CQ Strategy, however, is learning how to apply knowledge about the intended target culture to other situations. Thinking cross-culturally involves mapping out the strategy of engagement using the knowledge acquired. Before I meet with one of the more than twenty ethnic Strategic Readiness Teams, I must take the time to re-adjust my thinking about the values and assumptions of the group, as well as the behaviors that might differ fundamentally from mine. Strategic mapping may give me the answers to some basic questions such as:

- How does this group regard the importance of this meeting?
- How much time should I spend in introductory "casual talk?"
- What is an appropriate segue into the actual purpose of the meeting?
- How much interaction does this group expect?

The answers to these questions cannot be generalizations. To be effective cross-cultural thinkers, we must remember that our interpretations of our observations could be inaccurate in unfamiliar environments unless one strategizes for these situations and encounters. The experience could be highly rewarding and productive, but confidence that it will be so is more likely when one has an array of options ready for application in a variety of situations.

Key Question: What do you need to plan in order to do this cross-cultural assignment successfully?

CQ ACTION (BEHAVIOR)

CQ Action (behavior) is where everything we've learned about drive, knowledge, and strategy is finally realized. Behavior is the only measurable outcome that can indicate whether one is maturing in terms of CQ.

If there is one word that describes CQ Action, it is COMMUNICATION. CQ Action is the extent to which we can manage our verbal and nonverbal actions in our relationships with other cultures to ensure that they are appropriate. If the other areas of CQ have contributed to the toolkit in thinking cross-culturally, then what takes place in our behavior will be a transformation from within, rather than a change of behavior on the outside. CQ Action is the cumulative effect of our drive, knowledge, and strategy.

In his book, *Leading with Cultural Intelligence*, David Livermore suggests a three-fold path to developing effective communication: 1) Adapt your communication, 2) Negotiate differently, and 3). Know when to flex and when not to flex.

Adapt Your Communication – Every culture receives information on different radio wavelengths and frequencies. Because of the different contexts in which all cultures interpret what is being said or not said, communicating effectively probably means changing one's mode or style of communication. For example, the same speech or lecture that creates enthusiasm and vision when presented to one culture might instill lack of confidence and distrust in another, leading to alienation and a breakdown in future efforts to communicate.

In the Black church, one often hears something like "It's great to have Rev. Whoever and his lovely wife here with us today," which is nothing more than a traditional expression of warmth. However, in some cultures this seemingly harmless expression may be considered meddling or crossing the line into private affairs. Similarly, in some cultures it may be perfectly appropriate to inquire about someone's annual salary, and you would readily get an answer, while in other cultures, such as question is way off limits. In Black communities of faith, politics and religion coexist as instructive constructs for living the life of activist Christianity, but in other cultures, never the twain shall meet.

Culturally competent leaders understand that some topics are off limits for general discussion. Take, for example, several different ways to communicate a request to an employee. Which of these might you use?

- "Run the budget report!"
- "I want you to run the budget report."
- "How about running the budget report?"
- "Can you run the budget report?"
- "Wouldn't it help to have a budget report?"[122]

Of course, the one you'd choose has a lot to do with the preference for direct or indirect communication.

Negotiate Differently – Often, when a sponsoring congregation enters a relationship with a daughter church, negotiations take place that could lead to disharmony. Cross-cultural negotiations take into account the motivations of both congregations, as well as the manner in which each congregation interprets its mission and vision for the community and the raison d'être for its mission. Cultures view negotiations differently; in some cultures negotiations take place only after social friendships are developed and levels of trust are established, and in others they are handled as business transactions alone.

People from cultures like those in the US, Nigeria, and India, because of their cultural value dynamics, have a difficult time listening in negotiations, so a sure way to gauge the temperature of the negotiations is to ask open-ended questions. This slows the pace and creates space for deciphering clues, be they verbal or nonverbal.

In cross-cultural situations, we are never really in control. This is a hard fact for people from cultures that are highly individualistic. However, to be effective, one must be willing to give and take without straying too far from those values and ideals. The best way to determine the critical areas of flexibility is to revisit the cues in CQ strategy. Always be prepared to abandon assumptions that have not been rigidly ascertained as valid.

Know when to flex – This area is delicate because it is sometimes the expectation of the host culture that visitors act like those in the host culture do. It is difficult to determine how much alteration in our actions is necessary to be accepted in a culture. When is it okay to refuse to eat something that does not appear to suit one's culinary taste? This exercise requires drawing extensively on CQ Knowledge and CQ Strategy to anticipate what people from other cultures expect from us. On a visit to Kenya, a country with whose culture I was not remotely familiar, I had to be constantly aware of peoples' expectations. I was there with Nazarene leaders from eight African countries, each with its own cultural uniqueness. Questions that helped in this experience were those suggested by Livermore. How do these Nazarenes expect me to act, knowing that I am from the US? How do they expect me to act, knowing I am Black? How should their expectation affect my behavior? My answers to these questions undoubtedly affected my stay in Kenya.

Eight years ago I visited Hawaii with a group of Samoan Nazarene pastors. I was invited to participate in a meeting at which a ritual was being observed that involved drinking what I considered to be a libation. The occasion was one in which I hardly understood anything that was happening, but I had to make a decision to drink or not to drink! After one plea of ignorance when it was first offered to me, I decided to drink. Somewhere in that act, as I looked around the group, lay acceptance into the culture. It was as though I had accepted the rite of initiation. And I'm still alive, despite having briefly imbibed!

A warning must be sounded here. Some level of adaption within a culture is viewed positively, but a too-high level of adaptation could be viewed as mimicry and send a negative message. We need to adapt based on our CQ knowledge, drive, and strategy.

Here are some suggestions for effective behavior-monitoring:

1. Be aware of your own assumptions, ideas, and emotions as you engage cross-culturally.
2. Look for ways to discover the assumptions of others through their words and behavior.

3. Use all your senses to read a situation, rather than only hearing the words or only seeing the non-verbals.
4. Use an open mind to view every situation from different perspectives.
5. Create new paradigms/categories for seeing things.
6. Seek out fresh information to confirm or de-confirm new categories of experience.
7. Use empathy to try to identify.[123]

Key Question: What behaviors should you adapt for this cross-cultural assignment?

In his book, *Cultural Intelligence: Improving Your CQ To Engage Our Multicultural World,"* David Livermore suggests ways for improving CQ thinking for ministry in a diverse world. Here are a few salient suggestions:

1. Start the anthropological dig in your own soul. There must be a relentless commitment to reaching across to seek the welfare of the Other.
2. Root your view of the Other in the Imago Dei. See every person as created in the image of God. It is difficult to be entirely appalled by someone who reflects God.
3. Seek first the Kingdom of God. CQ cannot be compartmentalized. We do not embark on this journey to be politically correct; we are concerned about thinking cross-culturally because we, the body of Christ, are the language of God today.
4. Live up close. We are designed to live in relationship with those who see the world differently than we do, not to cloister ourselves with those who look, think, and act like us.

(Endnotes)

1. "Worship Across the Racial Divide," by Gerardo Marti. Oxford University Press: New York, 2012

2. S. Amanda Kumar, "*Culture and the Old Testament,*" in *Gospel and Culture,* John Stott and Robert T. Coote, eds. (Pasadena, Calif.: William Carey Library, 1979), 47.

3. Ibid., 89.

4. Banks, J.A., Banks, & McGee, C. A. (1989). *Multicultural education.* Needham Heights, MA: Allyn & Bacon.

5. Damen, L. (1987). *Culture Learning: The Fifth Dimension on the Language Classroom.* Reading, MA: Addison-Wesley.

6. Hofstede, G. (1984). National cultures and corporate cultures. In L.A. Samovar & R.E. Porter (Eds.), *Communication Between Cultures.* Belmont, CA: Wadsworth.

7. Kluckhohn, C., & Kelly, W.H. (1945). The concept of culture. In R. Linton (Ed.). *The Science of Man in the World Culture.* New York. (pp. 78-105).

8. Kroeber, A.L., & Kluckhohn, C. (1952). *Culture: A critical review of concepts and definitions.* Harvard University Peabody Museum of American Archeology and Ethnology Papers 47.

9. Lederach, J.P. (1995). Preparing for peace: Conflict transformation across cultures. Syracuse, NY: Syracuse University Press.

10. Linton, R. (1945). *The Cultural Background of Personality.* New York.

11. Parson, T. (1949). *Essays in Sociological Theory.* Glencoe, IL.

12. Useem, J., & Useem, R. (1963). *Human Organizations,* 22(3).

13. Peterson, Brooks, Cultural Intelligence: A Guide to Working with People from Other Cultures. (Maine: Intercultural Press, 2004).

14. Geert Hofstede and Gert Jan Hofetede, *Cultures and Organizations: Software of the Mind* (New York: McGraw-Hill, 2005), 4.

15. Pia M. Orrenius (2003), "U.S. Immigration and Economic Growth: Putting Policy on Hold," Federal Reserve Bank of Dallas *Southwest Economy,* Issue 6 (November/December).

16. Rick Lyman, *Census Shows Growth of Immigrants,* New York Times, August 15, 2006,

17. Michael Fix, Wendy Zimmerman, and Jeffrey Passell, *The Integration of Immigrant Families in the United States* (Urban Institute, July 2001).

18. U.S. Census Bureau, *Profile of the Foreign-Born Population in the United States: 2000* (U.S.Department of Commerce, December 2001).

19. E. P. Hutchinson, *Legislative History of American Immigration Policy, 1798-1965* (Philadelphia: University of Pennsylvania Press, 1981), pp. 492-520.

20. U.S. Census Bureau, National Population Estimates.

21. Oscar I. Romo, *American Mosaic: Church Planting in Ethnic America* (Nashville: Broadman Press, 1993), p. 41

22. This data is from Richard Harris, *The Planter Update* (Alpharetta, Ga.: North American Mission Board, 2002).

23. Romo, *American Mosaic,* p. 90.

24. Craig Kenneth Miller makes this observation in his article "Creating New Faith Communities," *Partners in Discipleship,* May 2004.

25. Jurgen Molten, *The Spirit of Life: A Universal Affirmation* (Minneapolis: Fortress Press, 1992), p. 146

26. Eric H. F. Law, The Wolf Shall Dwell with the Lamb: A Spirituality for Leadership in a Multicultural Community (St. Louis: Chalice Press, 1993)

27. Ken Crow, article published in Cultural Expressions magazine, How God Works Through Culture," June 30, 2010

28. Geza Vermes, Jesus the Jew: A Historian's Reading of the Gospels, Fortress Press, 1981.

29. Boice, James Montgomery. 1997. *Acts: An Expositional Commentary.* Grand Rapids, Mich.: Baker. P. 112.

30. The New Interpreter's Bible 2002, 110

31. Barrett, C. K. 1994. *A Critical and Exegetical Commentary on the Acts of the Apostles.* Vol. 1. Page 303.

32. *Wagner, C. Peter. 1994. Acts of the Holy Spirit. Ventura, Calif.: Regal.* Pp. 137-138

33. Internet Source, Grace International Church, http://www.gci.org/bible/acts6

34. John MacArthur, The MacArthur New Testament Commentary, Acts 13-28, Moody Press, 1996, page 61.

35. Warren Wiersbe, The Bible Exposition Commentary, Volume 1, Victor Books, page 462.

36. Donald McGavran, *The Bridges of God*: World Dominion Press, 1955

37. Ibid, p. 12

38. http://thoughtsofacountrypreacher.blogspot.com/2007_07_01_archive.html

39. Donald A. McGavran. Understanding Church Growth (Kindle Locations 761-764). Kindle Edition.

40. Donald A. McGavran. Understanding Church Growth (Kindle Locations 3313-3317). Kindle Edition.

41. Donald A. McGavran. Understanding Church Growth, 1973

42. Donald A. McGavran. Understanding Church Growth (Kindle Locations 3456-3459). Kindle Edition.

43. See Thomas J. Archdeacon, *Becoming American* (New York: The Free Press, 1983); John Bodnar, *The Transplanted: A History of Immigrants in Urban America* (Bloomington, IN.: Indiana University Press, 1985).

44. Manuel Ortiz, *One New People: Models for Developing a Multiethnic Church* (Downers Grove, IL.: Intervarsity Press, 1996), 29.

45. This is my paraphrase of Harvie M. Conn, "Foreword" in, *One New People: Models for Developing a Multiethnic Church* by Manuel Ortiz (Downers Grove, IL.: Intervarsity Press, 1996), 9.

46. We will be using some words in their original language to convey the ethos of our realities. *Caminar con Jesús* translated is "walk with Jesus."

47. Joan Moore, "The Social Fabric of the Hispanic Community since 1965" in, *Hispanic Catholic Culture in the U.S.: Issues and Concerns*, edited by Jay P. Dolan and Allan Figueroa Deck, S.J. (Notre Dame, Ind.: University of Notre Dame Press, 1994), 9.

48. Much of this narrative is drawn from Gabriel Salguero, "Multicultural Ministry: A Vision of Multitude." *Perspectivas: Occasional Papers*, Fall 2003, 83-91.

49. Bronx Bethany Church of the Nazarene, "Our History" at www.bronxbethany.net.

50. We are using the term American with a major caveat. If you are born in Canada, Mexico, Latin America, or parts of the Caribbean you are American. We would rather use the word United Statesean from the Spanish *estadounidense*. This word for many is a neologism but is a more accurate description of the realities of the Western hemisphere.

51. Eldin Villafañe, *The Liberating Spirit; Toward an Hispanic American Pentecostal Social Ethic* (Grand Rapids: Eerdmans Publishing Company, 1993), 102.

52. Ibid, 102-109.

53. Walter Brueggemann, *The Prophetic Imagination* (Philadelphia, PA.: Fortress Press, 1978), 13.

54. Latin version of Matthew 3:3, " I am the voice of one crying in the wilderness."

55. Please see Walter Wink, *Naming The Powers: The Language of Power in the New Testament* (Bassingstoke, Marshall Pickering, 1984); *Unmasking The Powers: The Invisible Forces that Determine Human Existence,*(Philadelphia: Fortress Press, 1986); *Engaging The Powers: Discernment and Resistance In A World of Domination* (Minneapolis: Augsburg Fortress, 1992).

56. Paul Tillich, *The Courage To Be*, 2nd *Edition* (New Haven, CT.:Yale University Press, 2000).

57. I am drawing heavily from Gabriel Salguero, *Joppa: A Shifting in Mission*. (Kansas City, MI: Church of the Nazarene Multicultural Ministries, 2006), Published sermon preached at Bronx Bethany Church of the Nazarene.

58. Samuel Carl W. Vassel, *Understanding and Addressing Male Absence from the Jamaican Church*, (D. Min Doctoral Dissertation, Columbia Theological Seminary/United Theological College, 1997), 54.

59. Eric H.F. Law, *The Wolf Shall Dwell with the Lamb: A Spirituality for the Leadership in a Multicultural Community* (St. Louis, Missouri: Chalice Press, 1993).

60. The term "other" has much significance we are indebted to Gabriella Lettini's Ph.D dissertation work at Union Theological Seminary on "Otherness.," see also. Levinas, Emmanuel. *Ethics and Infinity*. Conversations with *Philippe Nemo*, Translated by Richard A. Cohen. (Pittsburgh: Duquesne University Press, 1985); Emmanuel Levinas, *Time and the Other*. Translated by Richard A. Cohen. (Pittsburgh, Duquesne University Press, 1987).

61. Samuel Carl W. Vassel, *Understanding and Addressing Male Absence from the Jamaican Church*, 55-56.

62. Ibid, 55-56.

63. See also William Watty. *From Shore to Shore* (Kingston, Jamaica: Cedar Press 1981). 18-19.

20 Thomas L. Friedman, *The World Is Flat: A Brief History of the Twenty-First Century* (New York, N.Y.: Farrar, Straus, and Giroux, 2005). While we understand Friedman's thesis that globalization is making the world more interconnected we do not necessarily share his thesis that the economic playing field is being leveled.

64. Ann T. Fraker and Larry C. Spears, eds. Seeker and Servant: Reflections on Religious Leadership (San Francisco: Jossey-Bass, 2001), p. 89.

65. "2001 World Population Data Sheet," Population Reference Bureau 2001, <www.prb.org>

66. David B. Barrett and Todd M. Johnson, "Status of Global Mission, 2001, in Context of 20th and 21st Centuries, *International Bulletin of Missionary Research*, (January 2001): 25

67. S. Amanda Kumar, "Culture and the Old Testament," in *Gospel and Culture*, John Stott and Robert T. Coote, eds. (Pasadena, Calif.: William Carey Library, 1979), 47.

68. Ibid., 89.

69. Peterson, Brooks, Cultural Intelligence: A Guide to Working with People from Other Cultures. (Maine: Intercultural Press, 2004).

70. Geert Hofstede and Gert Jan Hofetede, *Cultures and Organizations: Software of the Mind* (New York: McGraw-Hill, 2005), 4.

71. Soon Ang and Linn Van Dyne, "Conceptualization of Cultural Intelligence" in *Handbook of Cultural Intelligence: Theory, Measurement, and Applications* (Armonk, NY: M.E. Sharpe, 2008), 3.

72. Ferraro, Gary. *The Cultural Dimension of International Business*, 5th Edition. (Upper Saddle River, NJ: Prentice-Hall, 2006), 12.

73. Economist Intelligence Unit. *CEO Briefing: Corporate Priorities for 2006 and beyond*. The Economist: Economic Intelligence Unit.

74. Livermore, David. The Cultural Intelligence Difference. (New York: AMACOM, 2011), 10-11.

75. Duane Elmer. Cross-Cultural Servanthood: Serving the World in Christlike Humility (pp. 126-127). Kindle Edition.

76. http://www.kwintessential.co.uk/cultural-services/articles/crosscultural-marketing.html

77. Livermore, David. The Cultural Intelligence Difference (New York: AMACOM, 2011), p. 89.

78. Ibid, p. 89.

79. Ibid, p. 90.

80. Ibid, p. 90.

81. Ibid. p. 91

82. Ibid, p. 92.

83. Ibid, p. 92.

84. P. Christopher Earley, Soon Ang, and Joo-Seng Tan. *CQ: Developing Cultural Intelligence at Work* (Stanford, CA: Stanford Business Books, 2006), p. 44

85. P. Christopher Earley and Soon Ang, Cultural Intelligence: Individual Interactions Across Cultures (Stanford, Calif.: Stanford Business Books, 2003).

86. Livermore, David. The Cultural Intelligence Difference

87. The web site should be used for further reference: http://www.kissboworshakehands.com/2004GTC/index.html

88. P. Christopher Earley and Soon Ang, 2003.

89. On-line Cross-Cultural Resources -- http://www.kwintessential.co.uk/cultural-services/articles-intercultural.html

90. Duane Elmer. Cross-Cultural Connections: Stepping Out and Fitting in Around the World (p. 40). Kindle Edition.

91. Summarized and adapted from Duane Elmer's recounting of this story: Cross-Cultural Conflict. Building Relationships for Effective Ministry (Downers Grove, Illinois: IVP Academic, 1993) 113-115

92. Stefan Hankin, Lincoln Park Strategies, 2012

93. *Adapted from R. MacDonald, Three Minute Tales*

94. http://www.forbes.com/sites/glennllopis/2011/05/30/the-lack-of-cultural-intelligence-is-damaging-our-enterprises-and-our-economy/

95. http://www.businessinsider.com/ceos-need-cultural-intelligence-2012-10#ixzz2SJZm7wHD

96. Simma Lieberman's Inclusion Blog, Why Business Needs Cultural Intelligence, October 12, 2012

97. Christopher Early and Elaine Mosakowsky, Harvard Business Review: Best Practices, Cultural Intelligence, October 2004

98. Kerri Anne Crowne, Kelly School of Business, "What Leads to Cultural Intelligence?" 2008

99. http://globaledge.msu.edu/blog/post/1033/cultural-intelligence--asia-s-secret-weapon-for-international-business.

100. Lindsay McMahon, Under 30 CEO, Got Cultural Intelligence? Why It Matters for Your Business Success Abroad, August 5, 2012.

101. Anne Dammel's Blog, Global Business Advisors, Cultural Intelligence: Why Business Leaders Need to Understand It, 2013.

102. UC San Diego School of Management, Adapting to an Increasingly Global Business Culture, 2013.

103. Simma Lieberman, Alan's Blog, Five Ways to Build Cultural Intelligence, December 2012.

104. P. Christopher Earley, Soon Ang, Joo-Seng Tan, CQ- Developing Cultural Intelligence at Work. California: Standard Business Books, 2006.

105. Jonathan Birschall, The Financial Times, http://www.ft.com/cms/s/0/bd371350-0f2c-11de-ba10-0000779fd2ac.html#axzz2UjpiK4vn.

106. Merci Amba Oduyoye, The Value of African Religious Beliefs and Practices for Christian Theology, *African Theology*, 110-115.

107. John Mbiti, quoted in Kwame Bediako, *Christianity in Africa* (Edinburgh University Press/Orbis, 1995), p. 154.

108. David Barrett, George T. Kurian, and Todd M. Johnson, *World Christian Encyclopedia*, 2nd Ed. (New York: Oxford University Press, 2001), 12-15.

109. Earley, P. C., & Ang, S, (2003), *Cultural Intelligence: Individual interactions across cultures.* Stanford University Press: Palo Alto, CA.

110. Chapter appearing in the Cambridge Handbook on Intelligence, Robert J. Sternberg and Scott Barry Kaufman (Editors), October 2009.

111. Ibid., Sternberg & Kaufman.

112. Excerpted from "CQ for Cross-cultural Ministry Leadership" Assessment, adapted by David Livermore, developed by Linn Van Dyne, Michigan State University, and Soon Ang, Nanyang Technological University, Singapore, http://grts.cornerstone.edu/resources/glc/cqprofile.

113. P. Christopher Earley, Soon Ang, and Joo-Seng Tan, *CQ: Developing Cultural Intelligence at Work* (Stanford, CA: Stanford Business Books, 2006), 69.

114. Ibid., Livermore.

115. H. Richard Niebuhr, *Christ & Culture* (New York: Harper & Row, 1951), 29-39.

116. C. Kluckhohn and A. L. Kroeber, eds., *Culture* (New York: Random House, 1952), 181.

117. Howard S. Becker, *Art World* (Berkley: University of California Press, 1982), 133.

118. Geert Hofstede, *Cultures and Organizations: Software of the Mind* (New York: McGraw Hill, 1997), 5.

119. Edgar Schien, *Organizational Culture and Leadership* (San Francisco: Jossey-Bass, 2004), 17.

120. Clifford Geertz, *The Interpretation of Cultures* (New York: Basic Books, 1973), 5.

121. Rick Lawrence, "The 18 Month Myth," Group 20, no. 2 (January/February 2000): 24.

122. Adapted from Helen Spencer-Oatey's example of asking someone to wash the dishes, in Helen Spencer-Oatey, *Culturally Speaking* (London: Continuum Press, 2000), 22.

123. David Thomas and Kerr Inkson, *Cultural Intelligence: People Skills for Global Business* (San Francisco: Berrett-Koehler, 2004.

Made in the USA
Lexington, KY
20 December 2013